Patrick Snedden is a 50-year-old Pakeha who began his professional life in publishing after graduating in 1979 from Auckland University in accounting, economics and anthropology. He has been self-employed since 1984 and acts as a business adviser for Health Care Aotearoa, a primary care network of Maori, Pacific Island and community groups within the not-for-profit health sector. Since 1982 he has worked as an economic adviser to the Ngati Whatua o Orakei Maori Trust Board and he is part of their Treaty negotiation team. He has been a corporate director for many years and was a founding director of Mai FM, this country's first Maori commercial radio station. He now has roles in public sector governance. Currently he chairs the Housing New Zealand Corporation and the Counties Manukau District Health Board, and is a director of Watercare Services, a wastewater and water company for Auckland. He is also deputy-chair of the ASB Community Trust, the region's philanthropic trust. Patrick and his wife, Josephine, live in Ponsonby, Auckland. They have been married for 28 years and have five children and one grandchild.

PAKEHA and the TREATY

PAKEHA and the TREATY

why it's our treaty too

Patrick Snedden

RANDOM HOUSE
NEW ZEALAND

National Library of New Zealand Cataloguing-in-Publication Data
Snedden, Pat.
Pākehā and the Treaty: why it's our treaty too / Pat Snedden
ISBN 1-86941-683-X
1. Treaty of Waitangi (1840) 2. New Zealanders—Attitudes.
3. Race relations—New Zealand. I. Title.
305.823—dc 22

A RANDOM HOUSE BOOK
published by
Random House New Zealand
18 Poland Road, Glenfield, Auckland, New Zealand
www.randomhouse.co.nz

First published 2005

© 2005 text: Patrick Snedden

The moral rights of the author have been asserted

ISBN 1 86941 683 X

Design: Janet Hunt
Cover photograph: Archives New Zealand
Cover design: Katy Yiakmis
Printed in Australia by Griffin Press

Disclaimer

It is not unusual for a book of personal opinion to require a disclaimer, especially when the author has multiple roles in his non-literary life. So if the point needs to be made, then I will make it emphatically. All the material in this book, representing views both of substance and of error, is mine. Except insofar as colleagues may enter the narrative and be directly quoted in the text, none of what I have written in any way whatsoever purports to represent the positions which are or might be held by my colleagues in any capacity within any of the organisations, companies or institutions, both public and private, with whom I have a commercial relationship. These are my own views as a private citizen, not as a corporate director or a representative of any other organisation.

Contents

Preface 11

1 Growing up Pakeha Part I 21
   An ordinary life

2 Growing up Pakeha Part II 39
   Arrested development

3 Belonging and 'te tino rangatiratanga' 56
   Different sides of the same coin

4 Need versus race 70
   Dual world-views on the road to cultural recovery

5 Our stories are our way forward. 87
   The Tribunal is building a national legacy

6 Anatomy of a protest 100
   Lessons from Pakaitore and Maioro

7 A Treaty-based approach that works for us all.. .. 117
   Health Care Aotearoa and the primary health
   organisation (PHO) revolution

8 Reconciling ownership and mana 134
   Speaking past each other on the foreshore

9 Imagining the future with Article 2.. 171
   From Treaty truth-telling to Treaty fulfilment

Glossary 185

Preface

There is a photograph of my wife, Josephine, with our children when they were very young, sitting on the fenceline outside our house in Grey Lynn, Auckland. They are surrounded by our neighbours, recent refugees from Cambodia, and Naresh Soma, his wife, Usha, and their kids. Naresh is a third-generation New Zealand Indian whose family were originally from Gujarat province, and Usha was born in South Africa, grew up in England and came here after she and her husband married. Look over Jo's head to the right, and you will see affixed to the house a nuclear-free sign. The scene is relaxed, cheerful and inclusive.

When I am asked what it is to be a New Zealander, that image acts as a starting point for many of my cultural touchstones. God only knows what my forebears thought they were doing leaving Scotland and Ireland in the 1850s and 60s. In truth they had no idea what they were coming to, but they were clear why they were leaving. The religious, cultural and economic persecution was motivation enough to up stakes and leave, and to risk starting over in a country with people and customs not their own. In our brief occupation of this country as Pakeha this story has been told time and again, as migrants from all over the world decided that life in this colonial backwater was worth a punt.

Such was also the case for our Cambodian friends. They had left lives too ghastly for us to imagine, arriving without money, language, friends or local knowledge. Like my own ancestors, these people are cultural heroes. They have gone where few before them have been, and they have survived, and now flourish. Among these people I also count my friend Samadi, from Afghanistan, a government official who defected during the Russian invasion of his country. Through luck, guts and a lot of help from New Zealand friends, Samadi arrived here just over twenty years ago when there were no other Afghani in Auckland. A year later he was joined by his wife, Golbibi, and their seven children. On his first night at home with our family our four-year-old son sat on his lap and demanded Samadi read to him *Winnie the Pooh* — an impossible task, given his grasp of the language. Years later, he still recalls that simple demand as his first invitation to 'belong' in his new country. Now that family has five university degrees among its kids and the next generation is helping to populate our country. For years the local food cooperative of twenty families slipped in a couple of extra Kleensaks of vegetables for the Samadis. No big fuss. Just the ordinary kindness of decent people.

Declaring our house nuclear-free didn't feature on the US or Russian radar screen, but David Lange did. The extraordinary audacity of this New Zealander in addressing his opening remarks at the Oxford Union debate directly to the President of the United States created an indelible impression. The fact that we don't count in world affairs does not buy our silence. 'Punching above your weight' is a metaphor custom-built for New Zealanders and we let everybody know it, more often than not in a shy, unassuming sort of a way.

But it was the events of January 2004 that forced me to take stock of the nature of my own belonging in this country. How did I arrive, what authenticates my right to be here, what continues to tie me here, and how different am I from the forebears who preceded me?

Dr Don Brash's speech at Orewa that month fundamentally distanced him and his party from the idea of any on-going place for the Treaty of Waitangi, once claims were settled. His critique of Maori preference touched a nerve in New Zealand, particularly with Pakeha.

It was as if the time was right for a gloves-off conversation about our origins, our future and ourselves. As the talk began, especially in those early months of February and March 2004, there was an outpouring of angst about the state of race relations in this country.

For Maori, many of whom felt themselves to be the butt of this angst, this time was one of deep discomfort. When the foreshore and seabed was added to this national self-examination, there could be only one option for me. With Maori cousins on both sides of my family and thirty years of involvement with Maori communities in most parts of New Zealand, I decided I had to be in on this national discussion. Any experience I had gleaned could not be wasted. I was not prepared to remain privately agitated while publicly mute.

A speech I offered to my local Catholic parish community

of St Benedict's in inner-city Auckland became a public event. It provoked a series of invitations from throughout the country to speak to clubs, schools, universities and polytechnics, professional associations, church groups, hui and any number of other groups. It got me to places I hadn't been before and found me facing audiences of strangers that I would likely not see again. It was a fascinating interlude in my life, taking me completely by surprise, and I enjoyed it immensely.

In response to all these invitations I made two rules. I would only speak if it was a publicly advertised event, and there had to be plenty of room for discussion. Interviews with Carol Archie on *Mana Korero* and Linda Clark's *Nine to Noon* on Radio New Zealand's National programme and on the *State of the Nation* TV debate increased the interest.

At most of these talks I tried to frame the context thus:

> One of the characteristics of this debate is that it is less a matter between bigots and liberals, than one between those who are actively trying to understand our history and those who don't think it makes a jot of difference.
>
> It is also about trust, challenging the trust we have as citizens in our governing processes, as much as it is about trust between tangata whenua (people of the land) and tauiwi (descendants of all non-Maori).
>
> Critical to this is the matter of content and approach. I would encourage participants to abandon any form of slogan or attempts to malign people for their lack of knowledge. Rather we should encourage each other into a personal discovery of our own nation's history and make this discovery relevant to how we might act today.

I found this approach opened the audiences up, giving them the space to express their apprehensions and their ideas for change. In the course of a year I gave some sixty talks and spoke with some 6000 people, overwhelmingly but not exclusively Pakeha. As the talks became publicised I noticed more and more new or recent migrants in the audiences.

Much of this book is the refined output from those conversations as I tried to tailor reflections on my own experience in a way that intuitively addressed the issues of our own Pakeha 'right to belong' in Aotearoa New Zealand. Email became one of the great resources for commentary as I received feedback, not all of it complimentary, from people who had read my papers online or who were following up from talks they had attended. As the audiences stimulated discussion on new content, so I tried to anticipate where the next challenges would arise.

It was this interchange that focused my own thinking on what I came to believe was the pivotal point of our national debate. The starting point for this reflection had to be our own need to get to grips with the benefits of Te Tiriti o Waitangi/The Treaty of Waitangi for ourselves and for our country. Fundamentally, we had to start talking as Pakeha New Zealanders about our claim to ownership of the right to be here. Hence the title of this book: *Pakeha and the Treaty — Why It's Our Treaty Too*.

This text is nothing if not the hard-won reflection from argument and theory tested by the pushback of friend and foe alike. Like the New Year discussion at Hot Water Beach with Fran Darragh and her husband Russell Withers. They challenged me to examine more closely the Pakeha affection for the beaches. As a consequence of this I rewrote the chapter on the foreshore, to make sense of the contrasting personal connections we have as Pakeha with the collective connections intuitive to Maori. This contest of ideas was not uncommon. The dinner table at the home of Jim Kebble and Marion Wood on The Terrace in Wellington became a place to test my latest theory. Many did not pass muster. I took note of the public responses to what I had to say, keenly looking to adjust material that was too positive about outcomes or too cynical about obstacles. These public exchanges enabled me unconsciously to mine the audience for the insight that hard experience has taught. I encouraged listeners to turn on their 'bullshit detectors' as I spoke, and to critique what I had to say with passion, real examples and solid fact.

My continuous involvement with Ngati Whatua since 1982 allowed me insight that I could not possibly have gathered from academic study or arm's-length engagement alone. In no small way I have been privy to witnessing close-up the cultural renaissance of an almost defeated people, and I have gained some of the best friendships of my life in that process. Being part of the Treaty negotiations team led by Sir Hugh Kawharu made me a party to the almost forensic reconstruction of the history of Ngati Whatua. As more Aucklanders come to understand the contribution of this iwi to the city, their perception in the public mind has moved from being irrelevant or inconvenient to inspirational. It is the experience of Ngati Whatua that above anything else in this book convinces me that we are within touching distance of fostering a Maori transformation of enormous benefit to all New Zealanders. But to achieve this we must all face, and creatively deal with, the fundamental truths of our history;

and that history begins with the Treaty. This book is about identifying the elements of that challenge and suggesting from both analysis and hard-earned experience where the points of progress might lie.

Jenny Hellen, commissioning editor at Random House, enthused when I was uncertain and pushed me to meet real (rather than imagined) deadlines. Together with copy editor Susan Brierley she paid attention to the crucial details in the text. It was Jenny who insisted that I could not present these views without describing where they came from. Hence the mini life story in the first two chapters that open the book, 'Growing up Pakeha'.

If through this process I have become clearer about a common starting point for understanding what makes a New Zealander, it is simply this. You have to love the place, the whole place.

I did not think at the outset that writing this book would be such a celebration of friendship, but that is how it has turned out. Certainly the text would have been the poorer without the intervention of friends in crucial ways. But more important was the wairua which attended this journey. There were many reasons that I created for myself not to write, not the least just plain losing my nerve, but they were in the end unconvincing. The compulsion to finish came not simply from personal conviction, but more especially from the encouragement of friends who believed that these stories needed to see the light of day. So they have.

There was a moment in this journey, in the first quarter of 2004, when Josephine and I both recognised that the momentum around this race discussion was gathering steam of its own accord. I would need either to withdraw or to throw myself at it as every opportunity presented. We chose the latter path, and that was a hugely generous decision on her part. She had just started a new job, and she carried an extra burden with me often away, followed by many nights of being unavailable to her even when I was at home. Her support was immense, as was that of Alice, our one daughter who remains at home, who saw less of her father in this last year than she deserved. My thanks to you both.

The origins of this book lie within shared experiences with friends and colleagues whose passion is for a culturally inclusive Aotearoa that celebrates the Treaty as our founding rock. That passion is alive and well today. Like the roll call of founders of Health Care Aotearoa: Tariana and George Turia, Niko Tangaroa and Chris Diamond (who have since died), Joe Topia, Petra van den Munchof, Peter Glensor, Dianne Gibson, Jenni Moore, Rowena Gotty, Julia Carr and Don Matheson, Alayna Watene, Peter Crampton and Bridget Allan. These people have developed an organisation that works and is profoundly Treaty-based. It is now ten years on and their efforts show this is not just theory. I tell their story in the book, and it is truly inspiring. And of course the people of Ngati Whatua o Orakei: Hugh Kawharu, Grant and Rahera Hawke, Merata Kawharu, Joe and Rene Hawke and their family, Puawai Rameka, Rangimarie Rawiri and her daughter Rangimarie Hunia, Danny Tumahai and many I have known who have now passed on. There is nothing I have learnt in the bicultural transactions of my working life that has not first been experienced with these people who are providing contemporary witness of the power of the restoration of rangatiratanga. To get feedback from other Maori on my analysis I sought help from Kevin Prime and Rob Cooper, both Ngati Hine. They were gracious in their corrections and observations, and supportive of my endeavours.

When I wanted to check on the legal aspects of what I had written I sought out David Williams, legal historian at Auckland University and a major contributor to Waitangi Tribunal work, not least with Ngati Whatua. Don Wackrow, who also acts for Ngati Whatua in their Treaty negotiations, critiqued my grip of the legal questions and I corresponded with Grant Powell, counsel for Te Ope Mana a Tai, a critical player in the foreshore discussion. Suffice to say that while I sought expert advice from time to time, any errors are mine alone.

When I was losing my nerve I went to ask author and columnist Gordon McLauchlan to read the text. He hardly knew me and he no doubt has had this request many times previously. He agreed, and his advice and direction spurred me to completion. Without it, I would not have gone on. Dennis Horton, my former boss and editor at *Zealandia*, offered to review my drafts prior to their despatch to the publishers. Many parts he left untouched. Elsewhere with great skill he made the proverbial 'silk purse'. Since much that I have written about began during David Lange's tenure as Prime Minister, particularly the description of Maori renaissance, I asked him to look at it. He responded that 'with the effluxion of time, I had not done the facts an injustice'. I think this was positive.

Sending drafts to my family created some apprehension. 'Growing up Pakeha' was of necessity very personal. So too was the penultimate piece on the foreshore. These chapters had to involve other family members. While it was all right to expose myself as part of this task, asking them to participate required their generosity of spirit. They did not fail me, especially my eldest brother, Peter. We have not always been on the same side of these issues. So this book is as much a tribute to them as to any others. There are Maori dimensions in my family that show the strain and impact of the years of colonisation, where the struggle just to be who you were at times overwhelmed. Matters of whakapapa (ancestral connection) that joined both tangata whenua (people of the land) and tangata Tiriti (people of the Treaty) in our family continue to provide clarity for some and occasional confusion for others.

If nothing else, this book is an exhortation to all of us who live in Aotearoa New Zealand to celebrate who we are with unabashed confidence. No matter what our origins, we can be clear in the unambiguous knowledge that Te Tiriti o Waitangi/The Treaty of Waitangi continues to provide us all with the foundation for our joint home.

Patrick Snedden
Waitangi Day 2005

1 : Growing up Pakeha Part I

An ordinary life

Fire is my first memory. I was four when, with a friend, I lit a fire under my aunt's house, then ran up the street to my own place and lit a fire under my sister's bed. Fire engines arrived to deal with two blazes a hundred yards apart, while I watched from under the hedge opposite my home. Mum, pregnant and almost full-term with my younger brother Martin, was aghast, while Dad, recently recovered from a heart attack, was understandably livid. It was also my first memory of a whack on the bum. Suffice to say that when in 1990 my own house burnt down, my ailing father's response to the news wasn't overly sympathetic. 'Ironic, isn't it, son,' was his droll comment.

Understatement might be an apt motif of my early childhood. Looking back, it had all the signs of domestic coherence. The family comprised both parents with five kids

— four brothers and one sister, who was the second oldest. I was fourth in line. We lived in Mt Eden in Auckland for most of our childhood; our parents moved to Takapuna on the North Shore when I had almost finished school. Takapuna had been the family's Christmas holiday destination every year since the early 1920s, so moving there was a bit like going home. Dad was a lawyer with his father, and two of my brothers eventually joined him in the family firm. Mum was a full-time housewife, involved in all sorts of church and school activities. Our grandparents lived within easy walking distance and, up until my teens in the mid-1970s, were all very much alive. Both our grandfathers were veterans of the First World War, and were gentlemen in every sense. Cousins were numerous, and in the Irish Catholic tradition there were plenty of opportunities to see one another.

We boys were sports mad. Our closest mates of the same age were the Gascoignes, a Samoan family who lived near the bottom of our street, went to the same church and attended the same schools. They were good at rugby and cricket, and so were we. It was a near-perfect fit in interests, and there was no lack of combatants when any chance of a game was in the air. Rules were developed to advantage the home team, and changed capriciously at the drop of a hat if defeat threatened. No international juries here, or right of appeal. Any rule held, provided it was enforceable. Often it was the street that was the sporting field of dreams. Touch rugby and occasionally tackle on the tarmac tested the mettle somewhat.

Years later I would reflect on how important this friendship had been. The ease of our movements in and out of the Gascoignes' household, and they in and out of ours, gave us early confidence in cross-cultural relations. Their household followed fa'a Samoa (the Samoan way) but we never felt less than welcome.

Losing fear of the ball

Our childhood was not one of deprivation. Food was always available, and we had the same family doctor throughout my youth. The house was added to as the family grew, although there was a clear expectation that you shared your room — with the exception of my sister, who was obviously a special case. The neighbours were a diverse group. Across the road were the Sharpes, Australians who had settled in New Zealand, with two boys and a girl. The boys were of football age, went to Mt Albert Grammar, and the family was staunchly atheist. That didn't stop me collecting their tea coupons to raise funds for the missions, or selling them raffle tickets to support the Catholic schools. Mr Sharpe in particular enjoyed the contest as I tried to sell him the benefits of the latest raffle and he feigned determination to hold onto his hard-earned cash, which was not to be spent on Catholic folly. More often than not I walked away with the cash.

Next door, by my bedroom window, was a Chinese family with a trucking business and huge vegetable gardens. They also operated a brothel. Coming home one day in a taxi, I described where I wanted to be dropped off. The driver raised an eyebrow. 'Bit young for that aren't you, son?' Over the road on the corner was a poet, Mike Doyle, and his wife, Doran. They were great friends of my parents, along with the Drumms who lived just round the corner with their four girls, an added attraction for my brothers and me. Our section backed onto that of Mrs Bailey, our bête noire. A cricket ball hit over her fence for a spectacular six was a mixed blessing. The adrenaline rush of satisfaction at such a hit was quickly followed by a shot of cold fear as the retrieval process was contemplated. If you were small and the fielder, you were forced to follow the ball. Many a ball was lost and not chased.

On the leg side if you were batting facing the big tree and the hedge lived the Batchelors, a lovely old couple. He was a house painter and a patient man, not much interested in cricket but happy to have lively neighbours. We didn't see a lot of Mrs Batchelor, except when she was in her garden, which was prolific. She patiently returned our balls without protest. We always bowled from one end of the garden and batted at the other. When my sister watched her first cricket match, where my younger brother Martin was making his debut for Auckland against England, she was amazed to discover that bowling was done from both ends of the pitch.

Dad, who bowled leg spinners to us in the garden, had played for Auckland and his father had been captain of the New Zealand team. At weekends we would visit Pop Snedden and if the spirit took him Pop would come outside with a pipe and a bat and a couple of old cricket balls. Then he would proceed to hit the balls with some force straight at us. 'If you are going to be any good, son,' he would say, 'you have to lose your fear of the ball.' The process of losing your fear of the ball was equivalent to contemplating hara-kari at close quarters. But it must have had an effect, because while my eyes still worked I was a fairly good close-in fielder with good reflexes. He knew what he was talking about.

Pop Snedden was also a very determined and principled man. As a lawyer, he had a partner who caused a client to lose a small fortune. Rather than abandon his partner's client, Pop borrowed money, took the debt on himself and paid it off. He was also very tough; the partner didn't last. As a selector of the New Zealand cricket team he once resigned because due process around the selection of a player had not been followed. He regarded the law as both vocation and profession, and expected the highest standards from himself and his colleagues. Nana Snedden was also tough, with a wicked sense of humour. I remember visiting as a twelve-year-old, and kissing her on the lips while she lay in bed. 'You're just practising,' she said, winking at me. I must have blushed. 'I'm only pulling your leg,' she said, pointing to her own under the sheets. But she had no left leg — it had been amputated. She roared with laughter.

My mother's father, Captain William Quane, had been in the army and served overseas in Europe. He was wounded at the Battle of the Somme. Fifty years later I was with him on the anniversary of the battle when a *New Zealand Herald* reporter came to interview him about his experience. As I announced the visitor's arrival, my grandfather burst into tears. Half a century on he still had not enough distance from the event to talk about it without the associated emotional turmoil. The reporter never did get his story.

Pop Quane had been a real-estate salesman, a retailer and a builder. He was also a terrific athletics coach. I lived with him and Nanny Quane a lot in my youth. Their house was the same distance from school as ours, and when things got 'hot' on the home front I would disappear to their place for some respite and spoiling. Pop always had me on about the futility of team sports. 'What's the use of playing with others? If you win, it's because you all did well. If you lose, you may do well but someone else can let you down. Go for athletics. If you win, it's you who achieves the prize. The same if you lose — no one else to blame.'

Pop had some fascinating souvenirs from the war, like Lugers, a double-barrelled shotgun, a ceremonial sword, a gas mask and a German helmet. Many a time we dressed up and played war in the backyard. His was the car that I drove up and down the driveway in my first attempt at driving on my own. Trying to turn at the base of the drive, I miscalculated and pushed in the front left mudguard. I promptly drove the car straight up the drive and parked it. Nana was sick at the time, so she wasn't going out in the car, and Pop always got in from the driver's side. It was about a week before he noticed the damage. By then I was well gone, but he was savvy enough to enquire through my mother if there was anything I wished to tell him about the car. Like Saddam and his weapons of mass destruction, I denied all knowledge.

After Nana died Pop had a stroke that paralysed his left arm, but he was still agile enough in his seventies to help with additions to the family home, which he completed with the help of Uncle Tom, Nana's brother. Complaining was not a strong suit of Captain William Quane MBE.

Nanny Quane had been a teacher, and was one of the early temperance advocates in Thames. They used to hold their meetings on the top floor of one of the pubs in the town. She ran a very generous house, but knew how to stretch her resources. A survivor of the Depression, she had been a strong support to others in her extended family during those difficult times. Nana's porridge was thick, and you could stand a spoon in the teapot. She also had exquisite handwriting and was a stickler for making sure we did our homework. Every day Parliament was in session she sat and listened, and a photo of Michael Joseph Savage hung in the hallway. She was a great churchgoer and prayed regularly for all and sundry; I remember her as very tolerant and good natured.

Church, State . . . and sport

Mum was the central point around which the family functioned. Intelligent, enormously hospitable and independently minded, she managed us all with great common sense and still had time for community involvement. While many around her were caught in a kind of inflexible Catholic trap, she never surrendered her view of what she thought was the sensible course of action, regardless of the rule book. Her skill with strangers was legendary, as she had mastered the deft touch of introducing one to another with just enough detail to put people at ease. She was there with solace and sympathy when early relationships hit the rocks, and had a strong enough grip on all to hold us together when fiercely held views on the 1981 South African rugby tour were creating a family fissure. She died at 64 after five years with cancer. During this period I once asked her if she wanted to talk about dying. She responded wryly, 'If I do, it won't be with you.'

The Balmoral Catholic parish was a focal point of community activity. As a child at the convent school, the facilities I enjoyed were spartan. Nuns taught classes of thirty or forty children and discipline was swift and without appeal. But we learnt to read and write and spell and recite poetry by rote, had our elocution lessons every other week and went to funerals so often we were trained mourners by the age of ten. Every death was an occasion to avoid lessons, to hear the message of life after death until it was second nature and to grow accustomed to adult grief. If there was one experience that left me very well prepared for attending tangi in later life, it was this convent school exposure.

The Irish influence was clear and present in the teachers and the priest, but not many of us were truly recent Irish. Most of us had been here for several generations, but the community of interest was palpable. I remember only one incident in my youth when we had a Catholic versus Protestant stoush, and that must have been in the early 1960s while I was still at primary school. I think we Catholics won, but I can't be sure.

Secondary school was a whole new adventure. The school was run by Marist Brothers and was for boys only. The cane replaced the strap, but with one exception the teaching, if rugged, was generally fair and competent. The one exception was a young man who had taught only a few years in the order and, in retrospect, was clearly out of his depth. He had a temper problem and his outlet was beating the kids. It took adroit personal skills and threats of collective student retribution to get him to desist, but the matter was never resolved satisfactorily.

Sport was king at secondary school. Cricket and rugby, together with athletics, were all accorded high regard, higher in some senses than academic achievement. And that suited my temperament. One Friday when I was in Form Two I committed a misdemeanour of some sort, sufficient to warrant a caning. The teacher held the caning over until the following Monday — he was also the coach of my rugby team and we had a championship-deciding game on the Saturday; he didn't want his halfback injured and unable to play. The team duly won on Saturday, he got the glory of being the successful coach and I got whacked on Monday — with some regret on the part of the teacher, I might suggest, but whacked nonetheless.

By the midpoint of my secondary school days the world was experiencing major changes. The Vietnam War was in progress and all was not going well for the United States and its allies. The Civil Rights movement was having an impact in the States, and in Catholic circles the Second Vatican Council was signalling fresh new winds blowing through the Church. We were also on the cusp of the women's liberation movement, and birth control was widely expected to be accepted as official Catholic teaching.

Conversation had always been interesting around the family dinner table, and it was now becoming more pointed. My eldest brother, Peter, always took a major part. His wit could be devastating, and as I was more inclined to argument than most, I was frequently on the receiving end. It took me years to appreciate how good his training had been for me. Like my brother David, Peter played rugby for Auckland, and he was a real grassroots club man, a builder rather than a spoiler. So Springbok tours saw us at opposite ends of the spectrum politically. That was until after the 1981 tour, when he watched Donald Wood's film about the life and death of Steve Biko. This marked a turning point for Peter, and from then on he saw the football argument in a different light.

David had followed my father into law, and shared many

of the same ethical instincts as his father and grandfather. He has always been the one to whom family members gravitate to fix difficult problems. As I grew more involved in corporate directorships I became a frequent visitor to his office. As a family we trust his instincts and judgements. My sister Jenny was the first of us to travel overseas, winning an AFS scholarship to the US during her last year of secondary school. As siblings we saw this as a very exciting adventure, and she certainly came back with a significantly more grown-up view of the world. Teaching has been her vocation and she has been really successful, happy to stay clear of administration and be fully immersed with students. She has her mother's instincts as a reconciler.

Martin's life has been marked by success at cricket and law. It wasn't always the case. When he was dropped from the New Zealand cricket team after his first tour he complained about the unfairness of life within earshot of his uncle. A bad mistake. Colin, a former test cricketer and sports commentator, gave him a short, sharp lesson about taking nothing for granted, working for everything you achieve, and keeping your mouth shut in moments of adversity. As family interventions can often be, it was withering. It had its effect, however. Martin fought his way back into the test team on his merits and retired from playing at his peak, on his own terms. Cricket administration is now his great passion.

So within the family, Church and State were always under close examination, along with rugby and cricket results. Both my parents were great readers. Dad had a lively interest in theology and read widely. He was a good debater in private, but hated speaking in public, and he arranged his legal career so that he didn't have to go to court. He was also a very moral man. Like his father before him, he believed the ethics of the law took precedence over private advancement. He forswore ever being a director of a private company, arguing that it would conflict with his requirement to give unfettered legal advice. He didn't want to follow everybody's sports teams around because it was impossible to watch us all and he didn't want to play favourites. But if any of us got to play at Eden Park — as we did, particularly my brothers — he considered that an honourable exception. He would turn up, hoping we would not make fools of ourselves on this hallowed ground. Generally we didn't. Later on, when he was ill and dying, we had many conversations that reflected on aspects of his life. He was very grateful for his life and very proud of his kids. Not long after Mum died unexpectedly in August 1990, Dad told me he would be with her for Christmas. He died on Christmas morning.

The Vietnam War posed a challenge to family and Church. Young people like ourselves were generally opposed to the war and didn't buy the 'bulwark against communism' line. There was a volatile mix of race, gender, politics and religious change in the air. Things were freeing up, and this was filtering through to school. Simple matters like the length and colour of your hair, the way you wore your uniform, or whether uniforms should be worn at all were no longer just matters of school regulations, but issues of human rights.

Into this cauldron came the 1970 All Black tour to South Africa, and exposure to tough-minded discussions about racial prejudice. For the first time I was conscious that my schoolmates and I were getting into unfamiliar territory, arguing about race. I was sixteen and thought the issue was straightforward. The South African Government was imposing a legal system of apartheid that treated blacks and non-whites as subhuman. This was just the stuff that students at Catholic schools ought to be clear in opposing. I found myself receiving an early introduction to a more nuanced world, a universe occupied not by black and white but by tones of moral grey.

Becoming aware of 'being Pakeha'

At that time we did not have a strong conscious awareness of 'being Pakeha'. Our parents and grandparents rarely used that description of themselves, at least as far as I can remember. We just assumed that to be Pakeha was normal, reflexive and innate to all, and we held to that view with an uncritical confidence that our rules were everyone's, unquestionably. Throughout my schooling I never once went onto a marae. One of my classmates was Eddie (Eruera) Kawiti, a direct descendant of Kawiti, who had first opposed, then after much protest signed, the Treaty of Waitangi. Eddie's whanau have owned the land and glow-worm caves just south of Kawakawa on State Highway One for over 300 years. Nobody at school knew about this, nothing was ever made of it. The 'teaching moment' — an ideal opportunity to put some life into the Treaty on which our nation is founded — was thus never realised. Any distinctly Maori experience, reference to the environment or separate world-view was invisible. Instead, we went to the Waitomo Caves on school trips like foreign tourists.

The connection in my mind that might link a rugby tour to South Africa with an emerging renaissance of Maori in this country was, in 1970, still a decade away. I was not a natural ally for opponents to the tour. In 1965, like thousands of other Aucklanders, I had camped overnight outside Eden Park to get the first tickets to the final Test against Dawie de Villiers' Springboks. My grandfather and I had been in the crowd a month earlier, to see Auckland beat the Springboks and a burly, rough and tough Maori centre called Ron Rangi play a starring role in the defeat. To break the boredom as we kids waited to get our Test tickets my mates and I managed to take the hinges off the ticket door at ten in the morning and, to great cheers from our fellow campers, prepared to storm through the hole created in the fortress, free seats beckoning. We didn't count on the police and ground staff being wise to our trick. As the door came off we were met by a policeman and dog. Neither was smiling. The door was duly replaced and we returned to our place in the queue. The irony was not lost on me in 1981, when storming the ground during a Springbok game in Hamilton took on a whole different meaning.

A feature of the 1970 tour was the introduction to New Zealand rugby of the term 'honorary white'. Brown-skinned players on that tour were for classification purposes to be considered whites, so the rugby could go ahead without bureaucratic interruption. The farcical nature of the distinction was not lost on the players, especially when a couple of them were caught up in riots in South Africa and tear-gassed. The players left for their tour from the Hotel Intercontinental, on Auckland's Waterloo Quadrant. This was my first protest. It was aimed at making the players feel acutely uncomfortable about their choice. It achieved its purpose, but didn't stop the rugby. The All Blacks went, lost the series to poor refereeing, and Bryan Williams returned a superstar, an icon for black South Africans. If he could do it, so could they. But there was also a resolve, this time even among the rugby fraternity, that there would be no more tours with 'honorary whites' as part of the team. Unless we could all go — Maori, Pakeha and Polynesian alike — nobody would go. This, at least, was some small advance.

Debates about this tour had been fierce at school. It was the issue that got opinions steaming. Most supported the tour, on the basis that sport and politics were separate and that, anyway, the 'Boks' were overdue for a thrashing. Holding the minority position of opposing the tour on the basis of racial discrimination, while not comfortable, was not altogether lonely. Mike Treen, a classmate and later a foundation member of the Alliance Party, knew how to 'take it to the bastards', and we did a fair job of raising both the issues and the hackles of our opponents. As discussions go, a poll would have had us on the losing side. But the experience of sustaining the tension of the argument, and of having to marshal one's forces for when they really mattered, was invaluable.

University couldn't come quickly enough, but my consciousness of things Maori was still very scant. The Auckland campus was something of an education. Nga Tamatoa was asserting a very strong and separate Maori identity, Treaty-based at its roots. Though I was not involved, such campus activity was within my peripheral vision in my sober moments.

By June 1976 the All Blacks were once again due to travel to South Africa, and this time the nations of black

Africa determined to boycott the Montreal Olympic Games, beginning in July, if the tour went ahead. The tour was hotly contested within the rugby-playing population and the general community, and I decided to raise the issue within my own club at Takapuna. I was playing senior football at the time as a fullback and had come through the Auckland representative grades at under-18 and under-21 levels. Like all young players I wanted to go higher, and I had played invitation events for the Barbarians in Auckland. But I also wanted to make a stand about this tour. Chris Kennings, Auckland representative, captain of our senior team, a chartered accountant by profession and a thoughtful man, was just back from Montreal and had seen what the boycott had done for New Zealand's reputation, and he didn't like it. I had been looking for a senior club member to support the motion I intended to put forward at the AGM, that Takapuna should withdraw from the Auckland Rugby Union competition in protest at the All Black tour. Chris seconded the motion.

The evening of the AGM was like no other. Most rugby clubs would have been hard-pressed to muster twenty people for such an occasion. On this night the very large clubrooms were packed. All seats were taken, and people were standing in every available space. The chairman began by declaring my motion invalid, since it had not been received a full fourteen days prior to the meeting. This seemed to me a minor technicality and I suggested that as people had clearly come to hear the discussion it should at least begin, even if the motion lapsed. It was a rowdy scene, but this seemed a reasonable compromise. Though the motion couldn't be put, both Chris Kennings and I could be heard.

As I got to my feet, an idea came to me. As I spoke I began to point to individuals in the crowd, saying that if we were in South Africa today 'you and you and you would not be at this meeting'. The effect of this quite spontaneous device was to reduce the rowdy crowd to complete silence. The people I had pointed to were all brown. I then proceeded with my prepared speech, talking about the impact on rugby of our supporting the exclusion of our black and coloured colleagues from playing the game we loved and prized as an expression of unity among all people. Chris Kennings followed by recounting his experience in Montreal and the mixed emotions he felt attending the Olympics, when so many nations were absent because of our government's decision. At the end, while acknowledging that the motion was technically barred, I asked for a show of hands. Over two-thirds of the crowd indicated support for what we had to say, and some were on their feet, applauding. We had tapped into a common cause, not as an intellectual exercise but at a very basic human level, and we had changed people's thinking, even if only for a short time. It was a lesson well learnt about following your instincts and having the courage of your convictions. I had not long turned twenty-one.

By 1977 I had fallen in love and married Josephine Ayers, an anthropologist with a special interest in Catholic liturgy. We had met during my first experience of communal living at Newman Hall, the university's Catholic hall of residence. It was Jo who suggested that I relieve the boredom of a commercial degree with the leaven of some real thinking. I became unique for a small moment at university, being the only student to study accounting, economics and anthropology at the same time. It was just the kind of intellectual stretch I was seeking, but engagement with Treaty issues and Maori was still slight, except for the everyday interaction at the rugby club.

Meanwhile a friend suggested I might like to use whatever commercial skills I had learnt to support some work trust initiatives for the unemployed. Work trusts were a new venture endorsed by Prime Minister Rob Muldoon, aimed at getting gangs into work. My first task was to help a women's group in Mangere, South Auckland, who were designing and producing tableware with a Maori motif for the domestic market. The group were all Maori, aged from fourteen to about nineteen. My job was to help them cost the product in order to price it for retail. I suggested that as an exercise they run through the processes they routinely used to make their product, and at the end of the day we would measure the output and arrive at a costing. On my return I asked them to tell me what time they had started. There was an awkward silence that I put down to shyness. We discussed their work a little more and then I asked when they had completed the work. Again silence. It gradually dawned on me that these women could not read a clock. Long before the advent of digital watches, these women had gone through our education system and their teen years unable to tell the time.

It was a profound shock, and in retrospect a kind of personal cultural watershed. For the first time I started to ask myself questions about the differences that existed for Maori and Pakeha in this country. It was a destabilising experience and I needed some form of intellectual framework to make sense of it. I found my recently acquired skills in anthropology enabled me to find part of the answer. Practical experience was to go a long way toward providing more answers, as well as adding to the questions.

2 : Growing up Pakeha Part II

Arrested development

It was the occupation of Bastion Point in 1978 that really accelerated my new sense of inquiry about the Maori view of the world. The Land March led by kuia Whina Cooper three years earlier had been an emphatic statement. Maori had run out of patience over land-grabbing. What was more, they demanded a part in the future policy-setting in this country and they were going to muscle in if necessary to make the point. Bastion Point was an example of this. Joe Hawke and his Ngati Whatua whanau and supporters decided to occupy the Point in defiance of a plan by the Muldoon Government to subdivide and sell their ancestral land. The occupation, which would last for 506 days, was a crucible for Maori reaffirming their rangatiratanga, their right to be themselves. The message was clear and defiant. It also galvanised the debate around race relations, as daily the threat of political and legal intervention was being asserted and challenged. The personal cost of the occupation to the occupiers was huge, but mostly hidden. The divisions within the hapu were deep, with senior elders like Hugh Kawharu opposing the direct action, as all players struggled to imagine what the end game might be. It was fertile ground for Muldoon's famous divide-and-rule strategies. When eviction eventually took place, with a huge use of State force against the peaceful occupiers, many Pakeha may have felt a sense of relief. But many rational voices would also ask the question, 'Have we got this right?'

My own unease was growing and I started to ask about the history of this place, and to research the available material. Josephine and I were members of a small Catholic group, St Clare's, that was just forming, with a commitment to a more gender-inclusive, social-justice orientation than we had been finding in the ordinary parish. Bastion Point was thus a focal point of our regular discussions, though with our son Benjamin being born in late 1977 thoughts of joining the occupation were impractical. What was occurring, though, was a much more intentional examination of things Maori. The Waitangi Action Group was becoming visible, with disruptions of Waitangi Day celebrations a speciality subject. Donna Awatere, Ripeka Evans, the Harawira whanau with Titiwhai, Hone, Hilda and Hinewhare, Syd and Hana Jackson, Pat Hohepa and Atareta Poananga were among those providing intelligent challenge to the Pakeha perspective in a way that was often strident and intimidating. Their critique of colonisation on the home front was something every card-carrying liberal was forced to confront. University student life allowed for just this kind of self-examination.

The birth of our second son, Samuel, in 1979 called a halt to my Masters in Anthropology, with a thesis still to complete. Economic realities took precedence. My first job, as manager of *Zealandia*, a Catholic weekly newspaper, was a perfect fit. It combined the commercial skills of publishing and running a newspaper with an expansive editorial policy led by Dennis Horton, a gifted and incisive commentator. He managed to keep an essentially conservative church sufficiently agitated at the margins with a successful and interesting paper; and I got to learn the craft of publishing from experienced hands, while finding full scope for my sales and financial skills. The next five years was a very productive time.

The 1981 Tour took place during this period, and the choice of how to cover it was clear for *Zealandia*. We chose to oppose the tour, and when it proceeded, to cover it from a perspective of keeping watch on the State overstepping the boundaries of public order and control. Our Catholic opposition paper from Dunedin, the *New Zealand Tablet*, supported the pro-tour line of Prime Minister Muldoon and opposed anti-tour demonstrations on the grounds of disrupting public order. Our publication of photographs of the police batonning protesters dressed as clowns on the day of the fourth Test was among our most controversial decisions. The *New Zealand Herald* decided against running the photographs.

Our third child, Tomas, was born at home in the week of the last Test. We received visitors who were on their way to the protest, at the same time as family members were passing through on their way to watch the game. The tour split families, and tensions were understandably high, not just over the rugby. The weekly agitation was alerting much of middle Pakeha New Zealand to an uncomfortable reality. Here we were, prepared to take to the streets to improve the lot of black Africans, but we still had difficulty reconciling the Maori voices within our own country who challenged the received view of our own history. On the streets we were all of one mind about the black emancipation from apartheid, but we were morally grey about assertions of te tino rangatiratanga as an articulation of Maori sovereignty.

Bastion Point

The following year this emerging consciousness was put to the test as once again Joe Hawke and his whanau occupied Bastion Point. Prime Minister Muldoon had moved to have the Housing Corporation get on with subdividing the site, as first planned in 1978. This time Josephine and I were resolute, as were many of our small St Clare's community. We were going to support this occupation with our physical presence. We had done the research and knew enough about this land to know that the government had no legitimate moral claim to its confiscation. We camped up on the Point, and I met Joe Hawke and his wife, Rene, for the first time. They were grateful for our support and open in their generosity and welcome. It was the beginning of an enduring friendship. The occupation duly took place and many of us were arrested for trespass. During an interview back at Auckland Central Police Station a senior officer avoided using my name, referring to me as 'Red', the colour of the jersey I was wearing. Finally he asked my occupation and I told him I was executive manager of the Catholic newspaper *Zealandia*. He called me 'Sir' after that. The brief experience of a night in police cells was not edifying as I listened to one of my fellow protesters, a Maori, being bashed in the adjoining cell by our jailers.

The sequel to this was a court case where with nine others, including Rene Hawke and her daughter Sharon, we decided to defend ourselves. Rene proposed that I should be their defence spokesperson. My father took this as a serious blow — here we had in the family three generations of lawyers and I, one of the few non-lawyers, had decided to conduct my own defence! He sent my younger brother Martin, not long out of law school, to 'ride shotgun' at the back of the court. In the event a sympathetic and very able barrister, Mike Corry, offered support. He sat in the near corner of the court and as I cross-examined witnesses I would back my way into his corner and he would suggest the next question. This pantomime was played out for some time before a policeman in the foyer made a crucial error. He was the main Crown witness required to identify those whom he had arrested and to point them out in the courtroom. I spied him going through a book of photographs and looking sideways at the line-up of defendants, prepping himself for his role of pointing us all out. I asked Mike Corry if this was allowed. It clearly was not, so I immediately called the policeman to the stand and asked him what he had been doing in the foyer. He knew he was caught and acknowledged his error. The judge dismissed all the charges against everyone but me. He reasoned that as everyone in the court had been referring to the defence counsel as Mr Snedden, my identity was not in question and no further evidential proof was required.

I was duly convicted for trespass and fined $120. Dennis Horton, *Zealandia*'s editor and my boss, paid my fine. Martin reported back to my father that, as a non-lawyer, getting nine out of ten off the charge was smart work — even if I had failed on my own account.

Not long after the court case Joe Hawke asked me if I would help his hapu in getting some forms of economic development off the ground. Employment training schemes were our first initiative, and this began an on-going association with Ngati Whatua at Orakei that still exists today.

Joe Hawke is an extraordinary New Zealander. With the occupation of Bastion Point he and his whanau risked the ire and experienced the economic sanction of a hostile New Zealand public. For years after the occupation he was unemployable, the growing family supported by Rene's astute financial and management skills. Yet under Joe's leadership the cause was intelligently and resolutely prosecuted until he achieved just and appropriate recognition, with the 1987 Waitangi Tribunal finding in favour of Ngati Whatua. On a personal note, Joe and his family and all those who were arrested for protesting found little comfort. He had asked the Tribunal to pardon all those involved. The Tribunal felt it was not within its powers to do this, although it noted:

> ... the stand at Bastion Point was the culmination of over 100 years of continued representations made only through appropriate channels. These representations and actions were futile for Ngati Whatua, and yet there is a long history of breaches of the Treaty, breaches that turned a proud and loyal tribe into virtual refugees — a disillusioned, scattered and landless people. Any illegalities

in the protest should be weighed with the enormity of the Ngati Whatua loss and the need, seen then as compelling, to call a stop to what was happening.

The Tribunal referred the matter to the Attorney-General, but to no avail.

Nevertheless the 1991 Orakei Act, supporting the public reaffirmation of the manawhenua of Ngati Whatua, would have been impossible without Joe Hawke's leadership and the sacrifice of his whanau and others of the hapu who risked public vilification to do what was right. When Nelson Mandela visited New Zealand in 1993 he spoke at a function at Auckland's St Matthew-in-the-City to honour the work of anti-apartheid activists who had helped his cause. Joe Hawke also spoke, about the struggle of Bastion Point. Mandela immediately recognised the integrity of Joe's narrative and invited him to share his car on the trip to Waikato to visit the Maori Queen. How often does this happen in our experience? So often the acknowledgement of a person's greatness is instantly recognised by a stranger, while the friend close by wonders what all the fuss is about.

Starting self-employment

In 1984 there was a changing of the editorial guard at *Zealandia* and I decided it was time to get into business for myself. A friend, Brian Healy, owned a monthly farming newspaper, the *Northerner*. He needed a hand to run his business, and he gave me an office. I began my own company, with Josephine and me as joint shareholders, and Brian as my first client. The company was grandly called Snedden Publishing & Management Consultants Ltd, a fairly ambitious stretch in anybody's terms, but you have to start somewhere. In the event this self-employment has been the catalyst for much creativity in our lives. It has allowed for the hard-edged pursuit of commercial gain while giving us scope to be involved in any number of not-for-profit activities consistent with our socially expansive instincts. This time also saw the birth of our first daughter, who we named after Merata Mita, the documentary maker who had recorded the Bastion Point drama.

My first year of self-employment was something of an economic rollercoaster ride. Labour had been elected to office, and Roger Douglas quickly removed price subsidies for farmers. Almost overnight the advertising revenue essential to keeping a free farming paper prosperous halved. We and the *Northener* nearly collapsed financially, but in fact recovered to expand the paper and sell it in 1987 to Mike Robson at INL for a tidy sum. By then I was a shareholder and so reaped some of the gain. This was also the time when Josephine and I began, with Ron and Alison O'Grady as editors, an ecumenical social issues magazine called *Accent Magazine*. Politics, race relations, economics, theology, arts and culture were the staple diet of this monthly and it remained in circulation for three years. It was the first of the community publications that were to become the base of a much larger publishing venture, begun in 1989 with new partners. This company, Snedden & Cervin Publishing, became a leader in data-based publications for educational and medical clients, here and in Australia. We sold our interests in it in 1999.

Labour was also in reforming social mode. At the prompting of Matiu Rata the mandate of the Waitangi

Tribunal was extended in early 1985, and claims were now able to be lodged dealing with grievances related to potential Treaty breaches dating back to 1840. The impact of this on Maori was formidable. One of the earliest claims (Wai 9) was launched by Joe Hawke, and vindication was won by Ngati Whatua in 1987. The Tribunal's decision was so unequivocal in its support for the Ngati Whatua claim that it boosted the confidence of Maori everywhere, enabling them to believe that here indeed was finally a forum that would take their history seriously. In a way not anticipated by the promoters, the result of such success was not simply to heal the past but to raise the possibility of ongoing constructive relationships with the Crown, which up to then had not been thought possible.

The beginnings of Health Care Aotearoa

At the same time as running the publishing house, I did work for Orakei and offered business consultancy for not-for-profit ventures. Most of these were Maori and Pacific Island-owned ventures, some were with unions, and many were in the health sector. Here Jim Kebbell was an inspiration, together with husband and wife Don Matheson and Julia Carr, New Zealand doctors not long back from a stretch in Zimbabwe. In 1987 they were involved with setting up and operating a union-owned community health service in Newtown, Wellington. It was immediately attractive to me as it combined many of the elements of community participation in its governance structure, with a clear focus on the health needs of low-income workers and beneficiaries. Jim, who had not long exited the Catholic priesthood, got me involved to help construct a commercially successful business model. Local doctors bitterly opposed the service because they viewed it as unfair competition, and saw the salaried employment of their colleagues as a foreshadowing of the nationalisation of the primary health sector.

This was one of the first two primary health services of a national network called Health Care Aotearoa Inc. There are now fifty-five of these services, serving 150,000 people nationwide, and half of these services are Maori owned and operated. Newtown has been the model for many of the subsequent services. In 1994 the network employed Peter Glensor as a coordinator and retained me as a business adviser. I have been with them ever since.

Peter, who has a superb feel for the cross-cultural dynamic, is a former Methodist minister who spent time in Asia as a youth worker. He is also very well-informed on our own nation's history, a veteran of Treaty education within his own church, and a person never to be cowed in the face of tough Maori/Pakeha invective. He is proudly Pakeha, with an intuitive feel for the place of te reo and cultural interaction with Maori. In short, he is a well-rounded New Zealander. So I was in very competent company, being involved in the development of many Maori health providers from their inception. The media so often focus on the occasional public failure of Maori-owned and operated businesses and continually miss the success stories. Given that Maori have only owned their own health services from the early 1990s, their progress has been exponential and the positive impact on the health of their people is clear, if sometimes only to their own patients. The nation's appreciation of their progress is very low, and they are easy targets for the uninformed critic.

Jim Kebbell's wife, Marion Wood, was part of a group called the Waitangi Consultancy, offering practical commercial support for government institutions implementing Treaty protocols. Both Jim and Marion had run open houses in Wellington for people in strife. They were aware of the down side of life. Here I found neither illusion nor woolly liberalism. Debate with them was a sharp intellectual and practical contest. They were natural allies, hard-headed Pakeha businesspeople grappling with the same sorts of processes and challenges that interested me. Today our friendship has expanded to include mutual business interests in development and shared ownership of three organic grocery stores in the Wellington region under the brand Commonsense Organics. They also run an organic farm at Otaki, north of Wellington, supplying retail outlets nationwide with fresh organic vegetables.

A developing role as 'cultural broker'

Looking back, the die was well cast by 1990. Jo and I had had our last child, Alice, in 1988, so there were now five children and a mortgage of significant proportions. The publishing business was a full-time concern but there was no way I was going to end my involvement with Ngati Whatua at Orakei. I was thankful for intelligent and competent partners in Anne-Marie and Maurice Cervin. They ran the business in my frequent absences without complaint. My Ngati Whatua alliances were growing in ways I had not anticipated. Since 1982 I had expected to be given my marching orders as a Pakeha adviser at every tri-annual election of a new board. It hadn't happened. Hugh Kawharu (later Sir Hugh) and Joe Hawke, formerly on opposite sides over the 1978 occupation, were forming a rapprochement in favour of the wider interests of the hapu. The 1991 Act was to be passed and Ngati Whatua was to be re-enfranchised as holding manawhenua status in the central isthmus. There were opportunities opening up with Crown recognition. Joe Hawke suggested to the board that I be retained. Hugh Kawharu took Joe's advice, and there began a friendship and an association with Hugh that has become pivotal to my growing understanding of the need to make sense of the different lenses through which Pakeha and Maori see the world.

Hugh, an academic by training, who had studied at Oxford and Cambridge Universities, had been tutored by his grandfather's brother in Ngati Whatua history and tikanga. As a 22-year-old he witnessed Maori Land Court proceedings that saw the final alienation of the remaining land within the 700-acre Orakei block under the Public Works Act. The patronising and humiliating attitude shown by the Court toward Maori land owners had a material impact on his later approach to the Bastion Point dispute.

Although we shared a common discipline in anthropology, the forging of our friendship happened in the most unlikely of circumstances. The Crown wanted to privatise the railways, but there was a problem. Ngati Whatua had memorials placed on surplus rail lands, effectively reserving them to be set aside pending a future Treaty settlement. The Crown wanted to negotiate to clear the titles, so it offered the hapu a deal: 'Remove the memorials on the titles, and we will give you an option to purchase the downtown rail station [built on reclaimed land right in the midst of the hapu tribal area].' Ngati Whatua had no investment capital. The way the purchase was to be funded was by a consortium of Maori and Hong Kong backers bidding for and winning the right to build a casino in the railway building. If the bid was won, the casino operators would seek a long-term lease on the station and capitalise the payment for tenure in one lump sum, sufficient for the hapu to buy the land. However, said the Crown, 'If the bid is lost, so is your option on the land.' The risks to the hapu were high, and the down side of failure was to lose the opportunity to recover prime ancestral land.

One night, in an empty room at the deserted railway station, Joe Hawke, Hugh Kawharu and I worked with the trust board's lawyer, now District Court Judge, Chris McGuire, until well into the early hours of the morning on a document to facilitate the deal. The chemistry must have been right because out of that single shared activity emerged a camaraderie that dissolved any vestiges of distrust. The casino failed as an option, but Chris and I, now accepted as advisers by the Ngati Whatua Trust Board, joined their negotiating team to stitch up a deal that gained both the railway station and much more in later commercial negotiations with both Crown and developers. This will substantially underpin the hapu's economic development in years to come. But that is another story.

Friendship is never an easy process to describe, although we know when we have lost it. Hugh and I were separated in age by a generation. Once, as a wartime schoolboy ring-in, he had played cricket in a university team my father captained. His English education had provided him with a kind of linguistic polish distinctive to that ancient milieu, an accent that distinguished him from most New Zealanders. Along with his academic reputation it made him appear formidable, at times almost inaccessible. But chance is a fine thing, and we hit it off. I was interested in ploughing into issues of Maori concepts, thought patterns and behaviours, of both contemporary and customary practices. Hugh was from necessity forced into the world of business, property development, Crown negotiation and debt management. This was something I knew about. He saw the value that a role of 'cultural broker' might have in interpreting Maori aspiration within Pakeha cultural frameworks. Ours has been a relationship of unforced casual intimacy on these matters. It is an unusual dynamic that works.

The close-quarters involvement with Orakei through the 1990s was supplemented by lots of work with other Maori health businesses through my Healthcare Aotearoa connection. My experience with Tariana Turia and her efforts to set up Te Oranganui Iwi Health Authority in Wanganui was a salutary lesson in Pakeha obstruction, the kind described as institutional racism. Regional Health Authorities (RHAs) were at that time in charge of funding for the health sector. Tariana had already launched community-based projects, including mental health and drug and alcohol services, but she wanted support for a kaupapa Maori general practice. Numerous visits from Ministry of Health and RHA officials bore no fruit. Tariana and the chair of the health trust, the late Niko Tangaroa, wanted to do the haka on the doorstep of the health authority, so frustrated had they become. I went to see the CEO and tried to get underneath the delay and obstruction. Lots of words, but no commitment to action. The experience reached its nadir when a busload of kuia and kaumatua from the region arrived at the RHA on a hikoi, determined to show their unified support for Tariana's project (a matter that had been under contest). They were greeted by the CEO's personal assistant and told they would not be seen. With the best will in the world even I had to concede that what was stopping this was not the quality of the project, nor the competence of its leadership, but the racist attitudes of staff toward this tribal grouping. Not long after the hikoi the CEO was replaced by a new migrant from Scotland. One of his first questions was to ask his staff why Tariana's project, so well constructed and targeted to the highest health needs, had not been funded. The answers were not convincing. Within the month a contract had been signed and Tariana opened her new primary health service.

Once again, it took someone from outside the local context, carrying none of the parochial baggage that is so much part of our Maori/Pakeha interaction, to break an impasse by asking the obvious question and then taking the common-sense position. The insidious quality of racism is that it impacts on the ordinary aspects of everyday life. It is not the bold gestures of outright prejudice that are so difficult to deal with. In some sense these are obvious and visible, and their impact can be remedied publicly. But the official who files the application away, to be quietly forgotten; the committee that decides the idea simply doesn't fit the priority list; the implied consent when no one advocates for the more difficult proposal because the cross-cultural competence around the board table doesn't exist — this is where institutional racism does its work. It is the silent killer of trust and optimism, and it corrodes the possibility for a different kind of cultural interaction which is expansive, collaborative and respectful of the other. The blunt and awful truth is that in New Zealand this happens far too often for it to be accidental or acceptable.

In public life, it requires political nerve to take a positive view of Maori/Pakeha relationships that is more substance than style. I have always respected both Doug Graham and Bill English for the attitude they have taken to interaction with Maori. Sir Douglas was savvy and intelligent about restoring some balance to our historical relations, and a resolute advocate for the Waitangi Tribunal process. He held the ground within the National Party when many of his colleagues would have been pleased to see the Tribunal buried. He did so with grace and courage, and not a little cunning. He left office of his own accord, highly regarded by all as a superb and pragmatic negotiator. It was on Bill English's watch as health minister that Ngati Porou finally gained control of health service provision on the East Coast, including ownership and control of Te Puia Hospital. This did not thrill the Gisborne health authorities at the time. Here again was someone with a contemporary and innately sympathetic grasp of a capacity for Maori self-determination that could co-exist within the bounds of a parliamentary democracy. He also has the ability to articulate this view, no matter what the company. When National dropped Bill English as leader it was in part because he saw too much of the positive value in Maori being in control of their own affairs, a view that sat less comfortably with many of his peers.

At the turn of the millennium Ngati Whatua o Orakei took the decision to enter direct negotiations with the Crown through the Office of Treaty Settlements (OTS) to settle its Treaty claim. The process has been professional and exhausting. Careful research has been required to detail with clarity and vigour the impact on the hapu of land losses from 1841 to 1868. Many of the researchers have been Pakeha, as are many of the OTS staff. The fortnightly meetings will have gone on for nearly two years to reach agreement in principle. The practical reality of this discussion between Crown and tribal representatives is that it is detailed, pointed and occasionally tense. I feel privileged to be a participant in such ground-breaking reinterpretation of the founding of our nation. There is nothing reckless taking place here. Every paragraph in the historical record is being meticulously combed for nuance before agreement is reached. The difference is that both sides of the argument are being tested and litigated in the one forum. This history is not a history written by the winners. This is a history tested by source, scrutinised by serious scholars and inclusive of the Maori historical perspective, both written and oral. Yet most New Zealanders have no idea what is occurring in these forums, and therefore no idea of the positive impact such investigation and resolution are generating between Maori and the Crown.

The lost opportunity I saw here for the cross-cultural reinvigoration of our national story is one of the reasons I decided to write this book. I felt we needed to glean from this newly emerging historical record a kind of understanding that was missing from the discussion following the Orewa speech. It is important to give expression to a clear Pakeha perspective on what has been seen by most New Zealanders as a mostly Maori affair — our relationship as a people to the Treaty of Waitangi.

3 : Belonging and 'te tino rangatiratanga'

Different sides of the same coin

As Pakeha, often we don't know where to place ourselves. Yet we are clearly a distinct ethnic group — as different from Australians and French as Samoans are from Tongans and Tahitians. So why do we hesitate to identify ourselves as who we are?

A story may help to illustrate the point. One day I called a cab to go to town, but when I got in the driver headed off in a direction I didn't expect. 'E te alu ifea?' I said in my best and only Samoan. 'Where are you going?' He nearly leapt out of his seat on hearing this from a palagi, and we both fell about laughing. I asked how his morning had been. 'Busy,' he replied, 'taking people to the cricket test at Eden Park.'

'Oh, the Pakeha hui,' I said.

'What do you mean?' he responded, with eyes raised.

'Well, it goes on for five days, everybody gets fed at least twice a day, there's lots of controversy. For long periods nothing seems to happen, then suddenly people seem to be at each other's throats. In the end, they shake hands and mostly it ends in a draw. Sounds like a hui to me,' I said. The cab driver had the grace to chuckle.

Now there's only one place in the world where that conversation could have taken place and been understood, with all its cultural nuances. That place is here. If, like the cab driver, you can see the funny side, it's highly likely you belong here.

I certainly know I belong, and Eden Park is part of the reason. My great-grandfather, Alexander Snedden, was one of six Auckland businessmen who in 1903 purchased the swamp, drained it and turned it into a sports ground. Such has been our continuous connection over four succeeding generations that when members of our family played there, at either rugby or cricket, it was hard to escape the feeling that with this sporting whakapapa we had a home advantage!

Strangers in our own land?

Now not all Pakeha have this same sense of ownership about our country. Faced with Maori claims to indigenous status, many have felt like strangers in their own land. An alternative response to this Maori self-assertion is to retaliate, to assert our own form of Pakeha sovereignty. The need to claim our own legitimate sense of belonging in this country is close to the surface of our cultural sensitivities. Scratch it too hard, and the reaction can be fierce.

The South Island poet and writer Brian Turner articulates this raw sense of irritation better than most. Any kind of Maori assertion of cultural primacy that relegates his Pakeha ancestry and experience of living in the deep south to a kind of 'second best' is not to be tolerated. He asserts an intimate Pakeha connection with the land — a connection denied, he believes, by many Maori. Turner objects to the idea that because Maori have been here a thousand years, and by comparison Pakeha arrived only yesterday, Maori should deny Pakeha a depth of feeling about the land that is similar to their own. He disagrees fundamentally with the way non-Maori feelings for land and water are dismissed as less heartfelt, less sensitive, less spiritual.

So how do I as a Pakeha claim my sense of belonging here? Am I indigenous?

Well, emotionally yes and technically no. For me to claim my 140 years of direct ancestry is a source of pride, and this land is my home. But can I claim fairly to be indigenous in the same way as Maori, who have been here since around the year 1300? To do so would be to sideline over 500 years of Maori experience predating my forebears' arrival. What is more, my forebears were not the first people to settle here — an important element of the definition. So to claim to be indigenous in the same way as tangata whenua is unfair, and technically it is not factual.

But nor do I wish to tug my forelock in this matter. As Pakeha, we claim our belonging here through having descended from the settlers who agreed to the Treaty. The same Treaty that, by joint agreement of tangata whenua and tauiwi, gives all subsequent migrants and their communities the right to call this place their own. The importance of this cannot be understated. It was the Maori Land Court Chief Judge Eddie Durie who in 1990 first described Pakeha as tangata Tiriti — those who belong to the land by right of the Treaty. This is our unimpeachable security, our right to belong, passed from generation to generation.

On one side of my family, my migrant ancestors arrived at Port Albert near Wellsford in the 1860s. They became farmers. At the Port Albert wharf there is a plaque thanking Ngati Whatua for their assistance to the settlers and acknowledging that without that help they would not have survived.

Today our society is shaped by a set of cultural reflexes toward the land, our environment and the interaction between Maori, Pakeha and Pacific peoples that exists nowhere else. Increasingly, our population is playing host to many new communities, and will continue to do so. The vast majority of tauiwi, and especially Pakeha, no longer have a bolt-hole anywhere else in the world to which we can escape, and where others will accept us as their own. I have visited the heart of my Irish and Scottish roots, and except for the most superficial acknowledgement people there did not see much of themselves in me, nor I in them. I am here in Aotearoa New Zealand for good, not only because I choose to be here but because I have nowhere else to go. And I am content with that.

Not all of us feel this comfortable, however. Many of us post-Treaty migrants still have emotional difficulty with our place as non-indigenous Kiwis. We know passionately and intuitively that we are not strangers in our own land, but we are unresolved as to how to describe ourselves. The subject is so sensitive that many of us want to drop the word Pakeha altogether. For others, the solution is to deny or contest indigenous status for Maori — 'We are all the same, after all.' Just being a New Zealander is enough.

I think we are missing an opportunity here. Being confident about our Pakeha selves will open up insights into the Maori world that we will not perceive if we are culturally on the defensive. Conversely, denying the distinct and different world-view of our Treaty partner will not satisfy our own need to belong.

This lack of cultural confidence often shows in our conversations today about the place of the Treaty. Pakeha — and, for that matter, many new migrants — look at the Treaty as being not ours but theirs, a method of leverage by Maori for resolving their claims. Once their grievances are settled, according to this view, the Treaty will no longer be relevant. How much more satisfying it would be if we all claimed and acknowledged our own sense of belonging — different but authentic to its core, and Treaty-based in its origins! Then this discussion would be quite different. The Treaty would become our Treaty, and our way of relating to the principles of the Treaty would be inclusive, not exclusive.

We need this confidence about 'belonging' if we are ever going to relax about the different world-views that sometimes separate tangata whenua and tauiwi. In particular, we need this confidence to deal effectively with the Maori view of te tino rangatiratanga. If there is one firelighter for Pakeha irritation, it is Maori self-assertion around rangatiratanga. But how many of us have any practical idea as to what this all means?

The Pakeha fear of rangatiratanga

Not long ago I attended the opening of a new marae in South Auckland. There were perhaps 500 people present, ten of whom were Pakeha. This was an occasion for the affirmation of manawhenua by the collective of kin groups known as tribes (iwi) or sub-tribes (hapu). This form of collective activity happens every day in the Maori world but, as I had cause to reflect, it is only tangential to the world of those who are not Maori. Here immediately we find some of the clues to our Pakeha puzzle.

There is a Maori world that operates within collective structures (iwi/hapu) and that has, at its core, expressions of rangatiratanga (chiefly authority exercising trusteeship) and manawhenua (tribal authority within a region). These collectives relate to other Maori, and to the Crown and its agencies, in a way not paralleled by any comparable Pakeha cultural institutions. They have been doing so since 1840. What's more, these collective structures exist in perpetuity. They are protected by Article 2 of the Treaty, which explicitly affirms and acknowledges this leadership of the collective (rangatiratanga).

If those opposed to the Treaty deny rangatiratanga, we must ask the question, how did we manage to get here? For it was precisely by exercising this collective rangatiratanga, on behalf of their tribal groups, that the chiefs consented to being party to the Treaty with the British sovereign. This was implicit in the Treaty trade-off. 'We tangata whenua recognise one law for all and the common right of citizenship, and you tauiwi agree to protect our tino rangatiratanga.'

Without explicit recognition of rangatiratanga in return for a single legal structure and citizenship in common, the Treaty would never have been agreed to in the way that it was. As tauiwi we have an obligation to protect rangatiratanga because it explicitly provided us with one law (Article 1) and the corresponding right of citizenship (Article 3). This being the case, why haven't we heard more about the Crown's responsibilities under Article 2? Here we touch the heart of Maori irritation with the Crown. Historically, Crown relations with tangata whenua in respect of its responsibilities under Article 2 have not been exemplary. Most Maori collective structures were largely ignored by the Crown for over a century prior to 1975, or dealt with remotely through the courts. Their presence has not therefore resided in our Pakeha consciousness with anywhere near the same force as it has for Maori.

So as a nation, when we come to pass judgement on the nuances of an issue like the foreshore and seabed debate, the Pakeha mind assesses the rights, privileges and obligations of individuals and assumes that this includes Maori. In contrast, the Maori mind goes to the rights, privileges and obligations of collectives, which to Pakeha count as extra benefits not available to them — a second bite of the cherry.

What blocks a more imaginative approach to resolving such cross-cultural misapprehensions? It is the Pakeha fear of rangatiratanga — or tino rangatiratanga, as it is most commonly expressed. What can this mean, we ask, if not a direct attack on the Crown's right to rule, the subtle undermining of the 'one law for all' concept? To solve this puzzle we need to understand something of the application of rangatiratanga.

In recent times it has been usual to juxtapose Maori

sovereignty with Crown sovereignty, putting each in direct competition with the other for precedence. It does not have to be so. There is evidence that the original intent of the parties to the Treaty allowed for joint protection under the law, but separate sovereignty over assets and taonga. If this was the case, are there examples of this working today? The answer to this is yes.

My experience at Orakei suggests that such an idea is not beyond us. Their story is about rangatiratanga exercised, lost and recovered. Ngati Whatua o Orakei, the once proud people of the Tamaki isthmus, who in 1840 held sway over the whole of Auckland, the people who invited Governor Hobson to Auckland to form the seat of government, were reduced in just 112 years to a landless few living off the State. By 1951 they were without a marae on which to fulfil their customary obligations, and were left with a quarter-acre cemetery as the last vestige of land they could claim tribally as their own.

In his claim before the Waitangi Tribunal Joe Hawke outlined the case relating to the loss of the 700-acre Orakei Block, the land ordered by the Court in 1868 to be forever inalienable, unable to be sold or transferred. The outcome was unequivocally in favour of Ngati Whatua, and in 1991 Bastion Point was finally transferred back into their hands by Act of Parliament. The area vested included the whenua rangatira now known as Takaparawhau Park and the smaller Okahu Park comprising the original papakainga and the foreshore.

In an act of extraordinary generosity, the first thing the hapu did was to give a huge chunk of Bastion Point back to Aucklanders. I refer to what is potentially the most expensive land, with the best views, in all of Auckland, the land where Michael Joseph Savage rests. Ngati Whatua agreed to manage this land jointly with the Auckland City Council for the benefit of all the people of Tamaki Makaurau (Auckland).

Controlling one's own destiny

What is it that enables a people who sought for 150 years to get some form of justice that recognised their cultural destitution to react in their moment of triumph with such generosity towards those who had dispossessed them? What underpins such an act of munificence? Put simply, it is the recovery of the hapu's rangatiratanga.

What has changed since 1991?

In practical terms, Ngati Whatua o Orakei are now once more in control of their own collective affairs, as defined and expressed through their own socio-cultural activities related to housing, education, health and marae-based activities. Substantial economic development is now occurring, especially through joint ventures where external finance and development expertise add value to hapu land. For Ngati Whatua, political relations have been transformed, with memoranda of understanding achieved with central and local government as well as with regional institutions and organisations.

The 1991 Orakei Act meant the full and unfettered return of their marae. The hapu has had the chance to rebuild their wharenui and improve their ability to offer manaakitanga (appropriate hospitality) to honour their obligations to others within their rohe, both Maori and tauiwi. This recovery of assets also provided the cultural space for tangihanga or burial rites for those who have passed on, a requirement absolutely fundamental to the mana of the hapu. It has also paved the way for a comprehensive Treaty settlement.

The social development of Ngati Whatua extended in the early nineties to agreement with Housing New Zealand as Crown agent on the transfer of ownership of one hundred state houses, with the attendant deferred maintenance and mortgage. A focus on educational achievement now sees the hapu claim tertiary graduates educated to Masters and PhD level across many disciplines, where before 1987 numbers with first-level degrees were in single figures. On another front, health services have grown to the extent that Orakei is today the most extensive Maori primary health provider in the Auckland region.

The potential for economic development unleashed by this statutory recognition of manawhenua has transformed the quarter-acre hapu of 1951 to one with significant land holding, including parcels of downtown Auckland. The Crown in this time has provided two separate allocations of funds. One of these, $3 million, came as an endowment with the 1991 Orakei Settlement. On a second occasion the hapu's Trust received financial consideration for lifting the moratoria on surplus rail land when the railways were privatised for Crown profit in the mid-nineties. The commercial presence of Ngati Whatua is now recognised in the marketplace as substantial and savvy.

Recognition of manawhenua reintroduced Ngati Whatua into the political and cultural life of Auckland via a structural relationship with the Crown and its agents. Such a reintegration is evidenced by Orakei now playing host to every significant dignitary to visit Auckland, including the presidents of China, Russia and the United States. This kind of public recognition had been almost entirely absent in their experience from the late 1870s. Successive generations of the hapu had seen their land and taonga disappear, and with it their tribal manawhenua, so critical to the practical exercise of rangatiratanga. Today, the restoration of mana is plain for all to see.

It is precisely this recovery that has reignited the capacity of Ngati Whatua to exercise rangatiratanga. An essential feature of rangatiratanga is that it relates to the group, not to the individual. In this respect the coherence of the group is evidenced by its size, its leadership, its marae base, its facility for manaaki and its relevance to other Maori groupings of similar kind, along with its political relations with the Crown and its agents. This has determined its capacity to exercise rangatiratanga. The hapu has reached a kind of cultural critical mass.

All this has been achieved without threat to the Crown's right of sovereignty. If this is possible with Orakei, why is it not possible elsewhere? I believe it is.

When the Treaty is working well, the nation prospers

Over my years of work with Maori groups and communities I have become aware of a central proposition. When the Treaty is working well, the nation prospers and is full of confidence. When there is fundamental strain between Maori and Pakeha, we lose vital momentum as a nation. There are plenty of examples where the mutual respect for mana inherent in the Treaty can be seen to lift performance and outcome for all New Zealanders.

Let me take you through three examples.

During my last five years as a company director I have been involved in two of New Zealand's most capital-intensive building programmes: the redevelopment of the waste water treatment plant at Mangere in South Auckland, and the reconstruction of the Auckland City Hospital. The combined budgets of these two projects amount to just under a billion dollars. Both projects have provided opportunities for the sponsors and tangata whenua to engage in constructive discussions to enhance the outcomes for all New Zealanders. The results have been stunningly successful.

In the 1960s, when the Mangere oxidation ponds were built, consultation with Maori was perfunctory. As a result the outcome was awful. Foreshore disappeared, shellfish were poisoned by toxic outflow into the Manukau Harbour, the birdlife vanished and the hapu, with its marae on the foreshore, saw its access to seafood decimated.

Today the area has been transformed. As part of the whole package, the rebuilding of the plant has seen the restoration of the foreshore and the enhancement of the environment for all recreational users. The birds and the fish have returned. It will soon be safe to harvest and swim again. And the Waikato hapu (Te Ahiwaru) at Makaurau marae has been intensively involved in the reconstitution of this wonderful piece of foreshore. This was not, in the first instance, an easy process. At one point the restoration was at risk of playing second best to the installation of an international rowing course and the pressure on the marae to agree was at various stages intense. However, formal agreements for restoration did, in the end, prevail.

How has this occurred? First because the Resource

Management Act required it, and second because Watercare Services, initially a reluctant participant, finally recognised that involving local Maori with manawhenua in this area from the beginning could only be advantageous for everyone. No big cheques, no scandals, just respectful understanding that Maori insight incorporated into the restoration of the environment adds a dimension that enhances the outcome for all New Zealanders.

Auckland City Hospital has experienced something similar. The rebuilding of the hospital provided an opportunity to think about how a Maori world-view on health might enhance outcomes for all users of the hospital facilities. So Ngati Whatua were involved at the early planning stages. They made a dramatic difference to the design of the mortuary, by introducing a place for families to gather with the deceased. They made simple suggestions about hospital design that provided for a 'tupapaku route', allowing families to remove a deceased relative from their place in the hospital down to the mortuary out of the public eye. This has been a great relief for all users of the hospital. The Maori perspective on respect for the dead has been embraced by all because it adds a dimension from which all can benefit. The hospital has clear and dignified signage in English and Maori, showing how to find the required services. Small but important symbols that show by their presence that living with dual world-views can be celebrated. It need not be feared.

A third experience relates to the work of Health Care Aotearoa. This is a primary-care health network with fifty-five providers nationwide, over half of which are Maori-owned services. The other services are Pacific-owned and trade union or community clinics. I have worked as a business consultant to Health Care Aotearoa since 1994, the year of its founding. This is a bicultural, not-for-profit network that provides first-level primary care for 150,000 patients, most of whom are on low incomes.

There are over three hundred staff employed throughout the independent providers, and they all sign on aware of the Treaty thrust of this network. For many of them this is a new experience. It is very clear that most Pakeha do not have the on-the-ground experience of working and living in circumstances where a Maori view of the world is just as important and as relevant as their own — and where, what's more, that view counts. In the Health Care Aotearoa environment the experience, however messy, is the reverse. Maori views do count and shape decision-making along with those of Pakeha, and the health outcomes for patients are steadily improving.

Some lessons are clear. First, a Treaty-based approach to managing our lives is possible and practical. Second, this approach can produce, for the most part, better results. And third, it need not be feared. What we have worked at in these last ten years to make ordinary and normal within Health Care Aotearoa is not replicated in the general community experience of Pakeha. And people without this experience fear it, or expect the worst.

Yet the reverse is my constant experience. So often, to do the right thing in respect of Treaty processes is manifestly to do the right thing for everyone. Time and time again.

It is not that applying the Treaty creatively and energetically has been tried and failed — it is more likely that this has not been tried enough.

4 : Need versus race

Dual world-views on the road to cultural recovery

Many Pakeha are increasingly uneasy about how Maori seem to have special status in New Zealand that derives from the Treaty of Waitangi. Our perspective is underpinned by a belief that this special status is supported by a raft of government initiatives based on race. So if funding for health, education or housing has any element that rests on ethnicity, as far as we are concerned it should be in the firing line. Talk to us about need, not race.

I suspect that what drives this is the iconic notion that 'we are all the same'. Yes, we have a Treaty, but it is an historical relic — a founding document, true enough, and an agreement that provides important and necessary ballast to our historical sense of self, but one that has no future. It is a document of a different time, and the world has moved on. It cannot be reconciled with the fact that today there are multiple ethnic groups here, and no one of these should take precedence over any other. We are, after all, a 'one person one vote' democracy.

It is unlikely that we would be having this discussion at all were it not for State funding, particularly of Maori initiatives. Remember 'closing the gaps'? This was quickly closed down because the Pakeha public had become alert to questions about money. Who is entitled to get it, we ask. Who is getting it, in fact, and who is paying for it? Talk of 'need versus race' suits us, because it is a clever slogan that divides those who should benefit from those who should not, and allows us to attack those we regard as undeserving for benefiting when they shouldn't.

Who could disagree with this? The argument is, at a slogan level, compelling, but it is also worth further examination. How well does it stack up?

Dealing with the facts — we are not 'all the same'

One of the advantages of having a seat on a District Health Board is seeing the evidence on which decisions are to be made. It allows a close view of this 'need versus race' debate, particularly in primary health care funding. It seems so simple: identify any health spending tagged to ethnicity and deem it to be race-based, and thus prejudicial to the interests of those not included. We are all New Zealanders, after all. Don't split us by race, and don't fund for difference.

The argument has centred over the establishment of Primary Health Organisations (PHOs) and the decision to weight the level of funding that goes to these organisations on the basis of the ethnic and socio-demographic mix of their patient bases. The greater the proportion of low-income, chronically-ill Maori and Pacific patients featured on the patient register, the higher the level of funding available to serve that population. Get this mix over 50 per cent of the patient register and the highest levels of funding are provided, mirroring the high level of 'access' expected by the government for this patient grouping.

With this decision under political attack, it seemed the simple thing to do was to address the evidence. In the face of the facts, however, the argument becomes more subtle, more complicated. Take the incidence of heart disease, one of the most frequent 'killers' in the population. Here it becomes clear that we are not all the same. An examination of the data shows that Maori and Pacific Island people have been dying earlier and more frequently from heart disease than non-Maori and non-Pacific Islanders. In fact, Maori men have been living barely long enough on average to collect their superannuation.

If this isn't stark enough evidence, the data showing just who has been getting access to life-saving coronary bypasses and angioplasty is not reassuring. On average, Maori have experienced twice as much heart failure and received less than half as many life-saving interventions as all other New Zealanders. This result is repeated in many other areas of high-risk health status, like access to life-saving cancer treatment. All this evidence is very easily available to anyone interested enough to make a serious enquiry. It is not, however, supportive of the slogan approach.

This evidence illustrates the complexities of any debate about public funding in which one group claims to be missing out in favour of another. The incontrovertible evidence related to life expectancy shows if you are Maori (or of Pacific Island origin) statistically your chances of living as long as your Pakeha neighbour are not good. At a personal level what the cardiac-intervention rates show is that the statistical likelihood of Maori receiving life-saving interventions is also low relative to their Pakeha neighbours — by as much as one-half to two-thirds. This is a startling discrepancy. It is a scandalous degree of difference, resulting in disadvantage causing death that ought to have any reasonable New Zealander asking, 'How come?'

So why, in the face of this kind of evidence, has the PHO scheme that will increase funding precisely to address this discrepancy been attacked as being race-based and not need-based?

The PHO approach allows for population-based funding. In short, when you go to see your GP, she gets paid not by the number of times you turn up (which used to be the case), but by having you enrolled on her patient register. This change means the government is now paying for GPs to look after a community (or population) of patients, not just individuals. The policy also aimed at ensuring that those with the highest need got access to this increased benefit as fast as possible. So in the first instance this funding went to the GPs who looked after the old, the young, the chronically ill and those evidentially most disadvantaged in health status (Maori and Pacific). In short, your PHO gets more money based on evidence of need. In spite of the overwhelming evidence in support of need, critics have claimed that because of the element of ethnicity in the formula, this money is being spent on the basis of racial preference.

The evidence demonstrates otherwise. In applying a population-based focus to primary health care, the government has realised that if it is to reverse the life-expectancy trends of Maori then perhaps the benefits of care are best delivered within a collective framework or ethic that is more intuitive to Maori. This is actually at the heart of the issue of efficiency. It means more Maori health providers. If Maori are to be helped to help themselves, this means supporting options to deliver their own care in ways most in tune with their own social system. It is plain, rational, economic common sense.

This kind of distinction over funding is made all the time. It is about the difference between equality and equity of access. We are not all treated the same. If that were the case, we would not have a pension system. We are clearly discriminating in favour of the aged when they get benefits that the rest of us don't receive. We are also treating families differently from single people. Families get tax rebates for children; single childless people don't. Treating everyone equally is thus not nearly as simple or as sensible as it sounds. A better indicator is equality of access. On that basis we pay the pension to the elderly because we acknowledge their right to participate economically in the fruits of society even though they no longer work. We also support the unemployed for similar reasons, although with a degree more scrutiny. Families get child-care support because we need the labour force to be flexible and active. We also offer to students loans that are not available to non-students. This is all about evening out an uneven playing field, and for the most part it gains wide public support.

So should it not make sense to guarantee equality of access to Maori for life-saving heart interventions? Should we not do more for Maori than non-Maori to improve that access? Of course we should, on the same basis that we pay pensions. We do so because we believe intuitively that Maori have the right to the level of life expectancy that non-Maori experience.

But as Pakeha, we know this is not just about equality of access or about money. It is also about influence, about who is entitled to hold sway. Who exercises influence so that university places are available in law and medicine? Who can hold up courts and tribunals, and on what basis, and who is missing out when influence is being exercised that is contrary to their interests? Many of us feel that the minority (Maori) are keeping us at a distance from the centre of power. That's why a powerful reaffirmation of the maxim 'one person one vote, under one law' provides us with a great way of getting tickets to the front seats, where we are back in control.

Tikanga — Maori and Pakeha

This is no more obviously the case than when we come face to face with 'tikanga'. The fact that hospital professionals are being required to learn tikanga best practice for dealing with their Maori patients is, for many Pakeha, a call to arms. If this is the case, they ask, why aren't they learning Somali best practice and Indian best practice as well? Otherwise, isn't this preferential treatment for Maori only?

So what is it about tikanga Maori that winds us up so much? Tikanga is about exercising your cultural manners in order that relationships are protected. Tikanga of some sort is practised everywhere every day by all of us, but as part of the dominant culture we Pakeha hardly notice because it is intuitive to our world-view. That is, until someone offends our sense of propriety. Last year Prime Minister Helen Clark offended Dr Brash's Pakeha tikanga when she refused to allow grace to be said and wore trousers at a function for the Queen. This was not a religious objection from Dr Brash. Rather, he was offended that appropriate Pakeha protocol of formal dress and the formal introduction of the meal was not followed, thus risking a potential slight to the sovereign. Importantly, the focus of his concern was the welfare and dignity of the guest, not the providers of the hospitality.

Now Maori are clearly comfortable that the Pakeha tikanga exists for the most part. They are capable of following it without undue compromise to their world-view. But in some circumstances they are clear that they must ensure their own cultural manners take precedence. This occurs when they are in their own milieu, such as on the marae or when the dominant agenda or kaupapa is Maori. It also most definitely applies in matters of sickness, or of physical, mental or spiritual vulnerability of any kind. The reason is simple. Without the protection that comes from attending to the wairua (sense of spiritual well-being within your kin group) the outcome for the patient, whether they live or die, is culturally compromised. Clearly a hospital is one such context in which an understanding of tikanga therefore makes huge cross-cultural sense. There is no treatment more patient-centred than ensuring the practice of sound tikanga.

Seen from this angle, it is something of a tragedy that after 160 years of living with each other there are still so few within the public hospital system who have confident and intuitive knowledge of such basic requirements of Maori. So now we have to institute a set of guidelines to help support and train them. It was not always thus. Early settlers and officials were relatively knowledgeable about things Maori. They had to be.

As to the Somali tikanga, many might be surprised at the extent to which public health systems are responding by way of translators and support people, and supportive reference materials for our new New Zealanders. Anyone giving this any kind of serious thought realises that this is not about special privilege. The simple truth is that we need to be able to understand one another in order to be able to function in respectful harmony.

If we look below the surface, however, we discover this is not simply a debate about manners. Just as with the reflexive resistance to tikanga, countering Maori influence is also about money, more particularly about cost of compliance. Monoculturalism is, by its nature, cheap and efficient. So when a taniwha holds up our highway construction, or a wahi tapu declaration stops us building a holiday house on the beachfront, this offends not only our Pakeha sense of 'oneness under the law' but also our notion of economic efficiency. This occurs regardless of the raft of legislation that provides legally for more than one view on resource consent matters.

Accepting different world-views

What challenges us here is the need to take heed of 'dual views' within our country and our world. For the most part, these views coincide. But as the seabed and foreshore debate has shown, there are times when the difference can be stark. When this happens Maori are attacked by Pakeha for holding things up, for not seeing things the way we see them, or for being unreasonable. Often this difference is portrayed as being not cultural, but religious or mythical — a private belief system, and not something the State should recognise.

The 'taniwha' example is an interesting one. For Maori, warning of the appearance of a taniwha activates a specific cultural metaphor that signals that a protection of a relationship is being breached, or is about to be breached. It often involves the prospect of danger or death. It is a serious matter, and serious attention needs to be paid to consequences. Right relationships need restoring.

Thus, when a stretch of roadway had seen repeated deaths from car accidents, tangata whenua were clear that the matter needed sorting. Except that such sorting required discussion, and perhaps a ritual response that in itself required a delay to the project, or even a redrawing of the road. The matter quickly became a contest between science and superstition, with a hint of commercial gain thrown in for good measure. What should have emerged as a constructive and appropriate contribution to solving the problem — death on this stretch of road — was reduced to a mismatch between the space age and the stone age.

But don't we as Pakeha find significance in cultural metaphors as well, even over roadways? Who among us has not seen the line-up of white crosses on the side of our roads, bedecked with flowers and occasionally inscribed with the names of those killed at this spot? What are these if not cultural metaphors? At one level they mark the simple passing of the deceased. At another level they sound a warning: be careful how you drive here. At yet another level, the use of the Christian cross calls down the protection and forgiveness of a God that looks over us. Agnostics can get a grip on this, even if they give it no credence. And what was the reaction in the Pakeha community when Transit New Zealand decided some of these crosses should be removed because they were unsightly and potentially 'distracting'. There was a public outcry. Why? Because people recognise that these symbols have a deep meaning in their lives and should not be trifled with.

So what is it that prevents us recognising that Maori might have a meaning system or cultural world-view different from Pakeha? What is it that stops us taking the trouble to learn the skills of negotiating these dual views with each other?

Part of the answer is that Pakeha are often at a massive disadvantage in these discussions.

When representing their own view of an issue, most Maori will be thoroughly conversant with the Pakeha view of that same issue. The reason is simple. For Maori since about 1870 onwards, exposure to all things Pakeha has been comprehensive and inescapable. Contrast this experience with that of the average Pakeha. We can live a full life in New Zealand and never have encountered Maori in their own milieu — be it at hui, tangi or on the marae. So when it comes to negotiating Treaty-related matters, such as resource consents where different views of an issue are legitimised by statute, we are often at sea and forced to seek and pay for Maori advice to make meaningful discussion possible. This is why the idea of 'countering Maori influence' carries such political traction for Pakeha. Because we are unable to tap this knowledge and influence, we become defensive. As the dominant culture, we find it hard to accept cultural vulnerability. The political promise to release us from such uncertainty has immediate appeal.

But have we more to lose as a country by not honestly confronting our own cultural deficit? Why do Pakeha for the most part lack the core knowledge that would enable us to foot it with Maori in their own milieu on their own terms? The answer lies in what we know about our own history. Often it is not much. For those of us aged 40 or over, an explosion of historical literature has in the space of one generation turned many of our cultural myths on their heads. Further, the detailed records of the Waitangi Tribunal, a bi-partisan tribunal, show a different picture from the education received by those of us born between 1940 and 1970. This is not universally popular.

For many of us there is a large knowledge gap. Most New Zealanders do not have a detailed understanding of the competing views of our cultural history. So when politicians say enough is enough to Maori asserting their Treaty rights, they find a ready ear in an audience prepared to live with a vague idea of historical injustice, but clear that it holds no contemporary relevance.

In 2004 Dr Brash was one of the most articulate of these voices. His stance was unusual because he chose not to contest the truth of the historical argument. From his viewpoint, the rewriting of history has but one strategic relevance — that is, as a convenient tool to settle and close off remaining Treaty claims. He will settle for a view of our past which shows that colonisation severely disadvantaged Maori in some places and that it often resulted in economic and cultural impoverishment. That's why the Tribunal has a role. It should get on with its deliberations, and enable the Crown to settle and finally tidy things up. But that's it. As Dr Brash said at Orewa in February 2004, 'Many things happened to the Maori people that should not have happened. There were injustices and the Treaty process is an attempt to acknowledge that and to make a gesture of recompense. But it is only that. It can be no more that that.'

Unfortunately, this is not good news for Maori who have settled Treaty claims on the basis that their manawhenua — their tribal authority within a region — has been affirmed. Explicit in those settlements has been the agreement that they will have a part in the shaping of the future of Aotearoa where the Treaty has a contemporary role to play. Negating this would be dire news indeed. Yet another agreement with the Crown may be about to be threatened because one of the contractual parties no longer subscribes and does not consider itself bound by its predecessors. This is very important. The policy of Treaty settlement is quite explicit that while the recompense offered is woefully inadequate as reparation, the future partnership relationships will help to assuage the uncompensated losses of the past. If tangata whenua were to lose that ongoing relationship with the Crown under a new administration, then the whole basis of the settlements policy would be undermined.

Celebrating our collective mana

Once again we seem cautious when in fact we may be far better served by a healthy sense of cross-cultural confidence in what we are quite capable — Maori and Pakeha together — of achieving. There is a word that evokes the best in this cross-cultural confidence. That word is mana. Linguistically its meaning encompasses the honour, integrity and respect that are integral to sound relationships, able to endure and based on authority. But the word loses something in the translation. Mana has a quality that is expressed externally, through cultural confidence; it is about how we present ourselves as a people and a nation, to one another and to others. Some may feel that at present our collective mana is at a low ebb, but over the last thirty years there have been lots of reasons to celebrate. Five examples will suffice.

The establishment of the Waitangi Tribunal

This tribunal, conceived by Matiu Rata and delivered by a Labour Government, was established in 1975 with a limited mandate to look at contemporary grievances. In 1985, under David Lange, its mandate was extended back to 1840 and the signing of the Treaty. It has had bi-partisan Parliamentary support up to now. This has proved decisive in race relations in this country. It has provided a forum — some would say a 'release valve' — for Maori who want their history recognised, their experience recorded, some compensation offered but, most acutely, their mana restored. Maori are hugely realistic that there is no going back to 1840. But they are also canny enough to know that affirmation of their manawhenua within their rohe gives them opportunities for participation in cultural and commercial affairs previously denied them. This restoration of mana, most notably by the defining of manawhenua, is extraordinarily important to tangata whenua but understood by scarcely a handful of Pakeha. Concluded settlements that define uncontested manawhenua give the holders significant advantages in terms of recognition by government institutions, the courts, local authorities and other Maori. The prospect that manawhenua could be relegated once again to a matter of no importance in the wider society is truly mind-boggling. Especially since the whole Treaty process turns on the understanding of being able to identify to whom indeed the Crown relates in matters of governance around its Treaty responsibilities.

The writing of our history in new ways
In this period of immense creativity, we have seen the emergence of major scholarship from Claudia Orange, Anne Salmond, Jamie Belich, Judith Binney, Alan Ward and Michael King, all Pakeha. They have taken a sober and hard-headed view of the historical record that first emanated from the pens of Peter Buck and Keith Sinclair. There are many others, both Maori and Pakeha, who have shaped the new written record through the histories commissioned by the Tribunal.

The approach of the courts
Required to articulate what an application of Treaty principles might look like, the courts have set in place working principles that successive governments have been able to shape to their political colour — that is, up to now.

The emergence of Maori school choice
There are now full-immersion Maori educational options, from pre-school to tertiary education. None of these existed thirty years ago.

The renaissance in Maori arts and performance
Undoubtedly the *Te Maori* exhibition was the most significant cultural export in expressing New Zealand self-confidence to the rest of the world during this period. It has been followed by an unprecedented take-up by Maori in the arts, producing some of this country's most significant branding in overseas markets.

An emerging cultural confidence

These examples serve to demonstrate that Aotearoa is a different place with different cultural reflexes from thirty years ago. The mix exemplifies an emerging cultural confidence on the part of all New Zealanders, a confidence that is currently under tension. That is why the focus on mana is so important. For Treaty settlements to stick, they require mana to be upheld — both mana Pakeha and mana Maori. Both parties have a lot to lose if the threads become undone. This means that future negotiations need to be conducted with some care, in the knowledge that reconciliation and closure have come at a price. And that price is compromise.

Maori have agreed by settlement, in fact, that a contemporary restoration to their position in 1840 is unsustainable, even though the gravity of their exclusion from the economic and cultural fruits since 1840 is conceded by the Crown. Often the most important value of the settlements is not the money. Useful as it may be for iwi redevelopment, this will quickly fade from memory. It is for Maori the restoration of manawhenua that carries clear expectations of participation as equals in shaping the future of this country, not as just one of many, but as a duly constituted founding participant of this society. This participation is as a full player, no longer a supplicant at the Crown's table. The Treaty process, so often derided by its critics as self-serving and encouraging a victim mentality in Maori, has achieved for successful claimants precisely the opposite effect.

The mana at stake on the Crown's side is what derives from the recognition by Maori that the Crown could have said 'No'. After all, it had for over 130 years. But through the Waitangi Tribunal, the people of New Zealand did not say 'No'. They said instead, 'Let's hear what you have to say, and let's clean up outstanding matters between us.' This is a breathtaking position to be taken by a dominant culture anywhere, and it is possibly unprecedented in modern history. People have talked in comparative terms of the significance of the Truth and Reconciliation Commission in South Africa. This came after the ending of apartheid, when the power dynamics had reversed in favour of the black population. We need only look to Australia, where 'not saying sorry' to the indigenous population has reached such absurd proportions, to see how far New Zealand has come.

It is clear that the Waitangi Tribunal could not have functioned without the consent of the population, the majority of whom are Pakeha and other recent or long-established migrants. In short, a lot of honour, integrity and respect has been put on the line to make this progress. These are not matters with which to trifle, whatever the short-term gain.

But as middle-aged Pakeha we do have a legitimate axe to grind here. This process has subjected our generation to a relentless forensic examination of the misjudgements and deceit of our nineteenth-century forebears. We find some of the implications of this newly discovered history hard to swallow. This new articulation of our past has, on the surface at least, unsettled our national centre of gravity, reducing our confidence in our cross-cultural future. We are suddenly nervous about what we might lose, forgetting for a moment the enormous lift to our mana secured as a just and open people through our support of the Tribunal.

This is something which those opposed to contemporary applications of the Treaty understand and are exploiting. We ought to learn the lesson. While we have been able to map accurately the historical misdemeanours of the Crown, we have not celebrated with anything like the same consciousness the recovery of honour owed to New Zealanders for consenting to this astonishingly open historical forensic examination. Nor have the leaders of successive governments been acknowledged sufficiently for their political willingness, on behalf of us all, to seek reconciliation and closure with tangata whenua.

The lack of attention to the successful settlements needs correcting, perhaps on an annual basis on Waitangi Day, typically a moment when our Treaty laundry is washed in public. Here is a chance to celebrate the closure that has been achieved and to retell the success stories of the fifteen settlements completed to date.

5 : Our stories are our way forward

The Tribunal is building a national legacy

A quarter of a century is not such a long time. The memory of the mood twenty-five years ago is still clear. Some said the country was on the edge of a racial explosion. Everybody was talking about Bastion Point and those 'bloody Maoris'. The government led by Prime Minister Robert Muldoon had deemed Joe Hawke and his whanau and supporters who were occupying the Point to be illegal trespassers. As the convoy of army trucks and police vans made their way up to the Point, cheered on by law and order devotees, some were already comparing this kind of State action with the moves against waterfront strikers in 1951.

The propaganda was relentless. Here was a communist-inspired occupation by dissidents with violence on their minds. The 'violent communists' turned out to be the young, the old (including members of the RSA), clergy and those rangatahi (youth) who had found, in their 'home' at the Point, their first real experience of being allowed to be Maori. In the event, the site was cleared of people and dwellings — victory with a clean sweep, if you believed the Prime Minister. But did the State win hearts and minds in this battle with its own citizens? History suggests otherwise. Maori imagination was stirred around the country. This clearance was only three years after the now famous Land March with its cry, 'Not one acre more.' The signs were now clear. There would be no more uncontested walkovers when Maori interests were at stake.

Standing atop Bastion Point today, close by the Michael Joseph Savage memorial and overlooking the magnificent Waitemata Harbour, most of us find it difficult to conjure up the strife this place has seen, unless we were part of the story. This rather sums up our national dilemma over the interaction of Maori and Pakeha. Whenever strife takes place the nation is riveted, just as it was in 1978. When resolution occurs, formally represented in this case by the passing of the 1991 Orakei Act, it receives five minutes of national news time and that's the end of the matter. Time and again the opportunity for retelling the stories and for mature reflection on the successful resolution of our disputes is lost.

I had an experience like this in Nelson. Over 150 people had gathered for a discussion on the foreshore and seabed issue. The audience was middle-aged and older, Pakeha for the most part, and clearly interested in becoming informed and doing the right thing. I asked for a show of hands to indicate the number of people who had read the Ngai Tahu settlement story. Hardly a hand rose. These were typical

New Zealanders, an intelligent group, replete with goodwill but desperately short of some of the basic information that could inform this particular discussion.

The challenge to redress this knowledge deficit is simply fundamental to the reasonable repair of our race relations. How much better off the ordinary New Zealander would be if they had received an understanding of the elements leading to that Ngai Tahu settlement. To know in detail the role of the Crown in the land transactions and to recognise in retrospect the kind of concessions made by the tribe to resolve the claim. This would give a new kind of confidence to all New Zealanders when we regularly address issues that derive from competing understandings of the Treaty. When we don't tell the stories, we don't get to understand the cultural nuances. Yet the stories of our nation's founding give us a real health check on interaction between Maori and Pakeha today.

Bastion Point is just such a story. But it makes more sense to all of us when it begins not with the 1978 occupation, but with the founding of Auckland itself. This is about the almost unknown tribal history of Tamaki Makaurau (Auckland) in which Ngati Whatua o Orakei holds centre stage. The re-emergence of this hapu after nearly 110 years of absence from public affairs in Auckland is one of the startling rediscoveries of this city in the last thirty years. How has this happened? To find the answer, we need to journey through three centuries.

'I did not sell it; I gave it to them'

In 1840, just months after the first signing of the Treaty, Apihai Te Kawau, paramount chief of Ngati Whatua, sent emissaries to Governor Hobson inviting him to come to Tamaki Makaurau to set up his seat of government. The government was weighing its options and at least three sites were under consideration. Apihai offered Hobson an inducement. 'Come,' he said, 'and I will give you 3500 acres to develop your settlement. Make this the capital, and I will give you more.' In modern terms, the area to be transferred is what has become Parnell, the Central Business District, Ponsonby, Grey Lynn, Herne Bay and some of Newmarket and Mt Eden.

Hobson officially arrived in early 1841 and was greeted by a gathering of 1000 Ngati Whatua on the shores of Okahu Bay. Ahipai Te Kawau addressed him: 'Governor, Governor, welcome as a father [matua] to me: there is my land before you ... Go and pick the best part of the land and place your people, at least *our people* upon it.' The block chosen was what we know as Westmere, Point Chevalier, Western Springs, Waterview, Morningside, New Lynn, New Windsor, Avondale, Mt Albert, Titirangi, Sandringham, Mt Roskill, Three Kings, Balmoral, Kingsland, Mt Eden and Epsom. This represented the transfer of a further 13,000 acres.

Why would Apihai have made such a significant gesture? What was behind his thinking? The answer was an alliance. The transfer of land was in Maori terms a 'tuku rangatira', a chiefly gift with strings attached. The strings were the advantages to be gained from commerce, education and health, and the protection of all under the law. The 1987 Orakei report of the Waitangi Tribunal commented that the 'settlers came not as conquerors, not as interlopers, but as Te Kawau's invitees to share the land with Ngati Whatua'.

All this contains a certain poignant relevance, for in 1868 at a hearing of the Native Land Court Apihai Te Kawau was asked, 'Who were the people who sold Auckland to the Europeans?' The answer was, 'I did not sell it; I gave it to them.' To the further question, 'Did not the Government give you and your people money for it afterwards?' Apihai answered, 'No, I have been constantly looking for payment, but have not got it.' Why was Apihai in the Native Land Court? Because within five years of the invitation to Hobson to come to Auckland, Ngati Whatua who had previously had uncontested standing as manawhenua across the Auckland isthmus had seen over 100,000 acres of their land disappear, with little to show for it. By 1868 they were reduced to the single 700-acre Orakei Block. So great had been the land attrition (most of it disappeared between 1841 and 1845) that Judge Fenton ruled the remaining 700 acres must remain forever inalienable, not to be sold.

The prohibition inhibited the State for a further forty-five years only. In 1913 the government passed legislation that freed the land for sale. While Ngati Whatua leaders were with New Zealand troops overseas, the government passed a law allowing for the individualisation of title. The land was sold off and what remained was a marae, a pa and an urupa based at Okahu Bay. Worse was to come. In 1951 the marae and pa were deemed an eyesore on Tamaki Drive and unsafe for habitation. The Auckland City Council as Crown agents evicted all residents to new state housing on the Kitimoana Street hill and razed the marae and surrounding buildings. The quarter-acre urupa was all that remained. Midway through the twentieth century the cultural devastation was thus complete. No marae remained, just a quarter-acre cemetery to stand as the last identifiable toehold in respect to tribal land holdings in the whole of the isthmus the hapu once controlled.

As a boy, Joe Hawke had watched from the hill as the marae was being burnt out in 1951. So when he and his wife, Rene, parked their van on the Point on the first day of the now famous occupation they had an advantage over most other Aucklanders. They at least had a real history of the land, passed through generations of their own people. But just about everyone else in the surrounding area, who were not Ngati Whatua, had no clue as to the significance of their actions. The beginning of the occupation opened up an opportunity for a history lesson for the rest of us.

Ngati Whatua were to have their vindication at the Waitangi Tribunal. In 1987 the Tribunal had heard Joe Hawke detail the case relating to the disposal of the Orakei Block, the land ordered by the Court in 1868 to be forever inalienable, but subsequently sold. The outcome was unequivocally in favour of Ngati Whatua, and in 1991 Bastion Point was finally transferred back into their hands by Act of Parliament.

'A benign but efficient regime'

This would have been story enough, but there was a quite remarkable sequel. As part of its settlement with the Crown over Bastion Point, Ngati Whatua agreed to manage the part of their newly acquired estate called the Whenua Rangatira jointly with the Auckland City Council, for the benefit of all the people of Tamaki Makaurau. This is how the Chairman of the Ngati Whatua o Orakei Maori Trust Board, Sir Hugh Kawharu, described the agreement to the Waitangi Tribunal, convened to discuss the foreshore and seabed issue in January 2004:

> Then from the trauma and the ashes the Crown restored title to Orakei's 150 acre 'Whenua Rangatira' parklands including the foreshore at Okahu Bay, forty years later in 1991. The Whenua Rangatira is now being controlled by the Orakei Reserves Board comprising three representatives of the Ngati Whatua o Orakei Maori Trust Board and three representatives from Auckland City Council. By statute, the land is managed, financed and developed at the expense of the Auckland City Council in view of the land (including foreshore) being kept for public as well as hapu enjoyment. Likewise, by statute, the chairperson (and the casting vote) is reserved for a Ngati Whatua representative in recognition of the hapu's title and mana whenua. The fee simple title to the land is registered in favour of the Ngati Whatua o Orakei Maori Trust Board.
>
> The arrangement has worked successfully and without untoward incident since its inception in 1992. This arrangement is incorporated within the Orakei Act 1991 and more particularly section 20 of the said Act. It is a benign but efficient regime; and here at least the mana of Ngati Whatua stands tall, intact and protected. In light of the current debate, I can confirm that public access to the foreshore of Okahu Bay has been unrestricted from the day title returned to Ngati Whatua. The universal celebration there at the dawn of the new millennium was an event I believe none of the thousands who were present will ever forget. And of course the beach continues to give pleasure daily to those who come and go.

> This is a model that the Crown might consider further in respect of foreshore and seabed policy. Here, at Okahu Bay ownership is formally recognised in favour of Maori, with the reservation that the foreshore and seabed are to be made available for the common use and benefit of the members of the tribal group and the public, and administered in accordance with an Act agreed to by Maori and the Crown. I have been privileged to have been chairman of the Orakei Reserves Board to date.

This illustration tells us much about an exercise of rangatiratanga that is contemporary and inclusive. Within the 1991 Orakei Act, all parties have negotiated a way into the future that is pragmatic and workable and profoundly Treaty-based. And everybody gets access to the beach, as has been our centuries-old custom. The relationship between the parties today mirrors exactly the trust underpinning Ngati Whatua Paramount Chief Apihai Te Kawau's invitation to Governor Hobson to set up government on Ngati Whatua land in Auckland in 1840. Subsequent events for over a century and a half showed that trust to have been systematically betrayed. It has now been restored by historic agreement with the Crown, and no one has suffered from the recent decision, rather, all benefit.

Achieving closure and moving on

The Orakei story is a story we ought to be celebrating as a nation. If we understood its significance better, we would be more equipped to address te tino rangatiratanga, the controversial notion at the heart of Pakeha apprehension over Maori sovereignty. The apprehension arises because

Article 2 of the Treaty of Waitangi, guaranteeing protection of the exercise of te tino rangatiratanga, has barely surfaced on the Pakeha radar screen, whereas Article 1 (one law for all) and Article 3 (common rights of citizenship) fit easily into our twenty-first century sense of nationhood. When Article 2 appears, it is almost always from Maori advocacy, and often with a kind of militant urgency. Treaty critics dismiss it therefore as profoundly self-interested, counter-cultural and separatist. In short, it is perceived as Maori pushing their own bandwagon.

But Article 2 is the pivot point around which the whole of the Waitangi Tribunal process revolves. It gives the 'pulse' to so much of the intensive investigation of our joint history, as the examination of alleged Treaty breaches reveals how much Maori capacity for self-management has been reduced. Ultimately the Tribunal has become a forum trusted for the power of its 'truth telling'. Its decisions contain a profoundly emotional resonance.

This quality of emotion is sometimes easier to recognise when it is not so close to home. Michael Moore captured it in his film *Fahrenheit 9/11*. There is a seminal moment in his film that is potentially illuminating of our Treaty discussion. It is during an interview with a black American woman who lost her husband in the Twin Towers attack. President Bush has yet to authorise the Commission of Inquiry. The woman is describing in simple and eloquent terms the gaping hole in her life since the loss of her husband. It is extraordinarily graphic, precisely because of the searing understatement. Nothing of the drama of her words is lost, and at the heart of the message is a plea, a call to action that is inescapable: 'I want some form of closure for this monstrous act. I want someone to accept accountability and responsibility.'

The Waitangi Tribunal has been our institution of 'closure and accountability', allowing for the patient, heartfelt, contestable and comprehensively forensic evaluation of our historical past. To date, there have been fifteen comprehensive settlements. These have brought matters of great pain and dispossession to an honourable and contemporary conclusion. Closure has been achieved through compromise by Maori and a willingness by the Crown to acknowledge historical Treaty breaches. Far from being a ritual genuflection to our uneasy past, the 'Apology' in each settlement accepts Crown accountability for this past. In doing so, it allows for the contemporary restoration of mana to all parties.

The parties can close the historical issues and move on. Such moving on, however, carries new rights and obligations. In particular, the recognition of manawhenua means that the Crown commits to dealing with this tribal group in matters that affect its interests for the foreseeable future.

I highlight the importance of these emotional aspects of settlement because of the status of our Treaty discussions in Aotearoa today. There is a solid constituency that wants an end to all this Treaty breast-beating. Pakeha are sick of being cast as the villains in historical accounts of dispossession. The past is the past, and what is done is done. In particular, the value of 'closure' represented by the Waitangi Tribunal's work is under pressure because, in the minds of some, this is all taking too long. Critics say it is continuing to provoke in Maori a kind of 'cargo cult' mentality. Hang on long enough as the oppressed victim, and eventually the State will come to the rescue with a cheque. For many critics of the process, the promise of a settlement tomorrow simply enables Maori to avoid personal responsibility today for their own actions and their own future.

In my experience, this is simply not true. What is happening with Maori throughout Aotearoa in these time-consuming, sometimes tedious, occasionally acrimonious and ultimately honourable endeavours is a genuine resolution of historical grievances. This is leading, in turn, to a resurgence of confidence among Maori when their truth is told and acknowledged.

But the process is under significant threat from two flanks. The first is the base level of funding for the Tribunal. We are making haste slowly because the budget available for efficient management of the workload is just too small. Even more importantly, some of the Tribunal's decisions are being challenged by the Crown through its Office of Treaty Settlements. Findings by the Tribunal are being relitigated in direct negotiation with the parties when the outcomes are not to the Crown's liking. This process risks undermining the value of the Tribunal to Maori who have seen their history validated within a forum whose decisions are contestable. Critical to moving on is that both parties demonstrate confidence in the process of resolution. Imperil this and we risk undoing the good that has been achieved to date.

However, it is also true that this 'truth telling' is nearly always overlooked when news of a settlement is announced. Almost without fail the emphasis is on the money, the commercial redress that accompanies the closure of the process. This is identified as the area of political risk and, especially in the climate of our current race relations, governments are keen to manage this risk downwards.

This is a matter of political leadership. Politicians of any stripe might manage this risk rather better if they decided to tell the people just what the settlement is all about. With every settlement there is an agreed historical account that leads to the identification in precise terms of the breaches of the Treaty suffered by the tribal group. As New Zealanders we need to know about this because it begins to fill in gaps of our history that hitherto have not been available to us. It has often been said that history is written by the 'winners'. In the case of the Waitangi Tribunal, both the colonised and the colonisers have sat at the same table and the historical account for the settlement is arrived at jointly and methodically — some might say, ponderously.

Many commentators continue to attribute to Maori the basest motives for settlement. Again, the opposite is true. Maori parties to settlement recognise that there is no going back, that commercial and financial reparation that would make good their historical loss in today's terms is no longer possible. Still this does not make negotiations a pushover. Discussions are often very difficult as both Crown and Maori attempt to manage expectations, knowing each has a constituency intolerant of weakness. But the balance of tolerance is exercised most patently by Maori iwi and hapu who have agreed that their proven historical losses cannot be recompensed, for to do so would create further injustice (such as compulsory acquisition of private land).

This is an astonishing concession on the part of Maori and, I might observe, one that is equalled at least by that of Pakeha in establishing the Waitangi Tribunal to begin with. I am unaware of any other country today where the dominant culture has provided for the forensic analysis of its indigenous history in the way New Zealand has done, or has acted on such an analysis to redress historical wrongs. Those who agitate to sew this process up as soon as possible, or to stop it altogether, misunderstand the fundamental gains achieved.

Our nation is reconciling itself to its past, slowly but adroitly, within an enduring paradigm that we have created uniquely for ourselves. For some of us, this may be acutely uncomfortable. But nobody has died from the discomfort yet!

6 : Anatomy of a protest

Lessons from Pakaitore and Maioro

Peacefully, before dawn on 19 May 1995, protesters left the former Whanganui pa site of Pakaitore (now Moutoa Gardens) after an occupation that had begun on 28 February that year. Like Bastion Point, this occupation was of national significance. It both galvanised and split the local community, with the majority being opposed to the Maori takeover of the park.

The presenting issue was a conflict between local iwi and the council and Mayor about ownership of the park. The iwi claimed it as an historic pa site of significance which had been taken, and which now featured statues that emphasised the successful colonisation of the local hapu. One in particular, of John Ballance, was seen as most offensive. The Mayor asserted support for the people of the town, who saw the Maori claim as threatening the quiet enjoyment of a public facility, which they had always assumed was there for everybody. For the occupiers, the issue was about more than just title to this piece of whenua. It crystallised their frustration over the glacial pace at which resolution of their Treaty claim was moving, a process that focused primarily on the awa (the Whanganui River). For seventy-nine days, as the drama unfolded, Moutoa Gardens became a media Mecca.

In considering our race relations, it is often instructive to take the long view. Matters that are 'white hot' for a time often come to an end unexpectedly, if not always completely resolved. As a nation we tend to be incremental in our solutions, only occasionally revolutionary in our praxis. 'Rogernomics' stands out as the exception.

So a decade after the occupation, what has been resolved at Pakaitore? To gain perspective on this question I returned to the notes I kept at the time. This is what I wrote then:

> You could be forgiven for being tired of the drama taking place at Moutoa Gardens. Readers and viewers alike must feel like famished explorers caught in the desert sun, with only bits of bread and water to keep them nourished. It all seems very tedious. But you would be mistaken. The occupation of the gardens is the story of New Zealand in the 1990s writ large. It contains all the elements that stake out our emerging nationhood in a way most of the media have missed, misunderstood and wilfully ignored.
>
> Wednesday night is wet and stormy. Indeed, driving through National Park to Wanganui the thunder and lightning appear ominously over the town. The rain is torrential, and winding 52 kilometres into Raetihi through

the descending mist is spine-tingling. This is a drive to endure, not to enjoy.

The welcome onto the marae is stunning. I and my passengers have joined a group of locals as our welcome begins at 8pm. There aren't many white faces around but lots of familiar friends from the iwi. This welcome is only one of a continuous series of powhiri that go on right through the night. The format is the same: the call, the greeting, the response, the sharing of the hongi and then food for all visitors. The mince, mutton and tea are welcome as it dawns on me that hundreds of people have been fed continuously, three times a day, for over ten weeks on this piece of land where running water comes from a couple of taps and a public toilet. The enormity of this achievement goes for the most part unnoticed.

But I am aware of much more. There's a difference here. A sense of peace and calm, so completely at odds with the news reports on the way down. The editor of the *Wanganui Chronicle* is quoted as saying, 'The town is sitting on a powder keg.' That may be the case in the town; it's no description of the marae, where there is a complete absence of tension. The reason for the calm becomes clear. It is the presence of so many elderly people, grandmothers, great-grandmothers, all the kuia out in support. Not just one or two but 20 or more. Here not just for a passing visit but living here, sleeping in the makeshift wharenui on mattresses spread out on wooden pallets that in turn rest on dirt floors, their only cover a tarpaulin that during the night springs many leaks.

The privations suffered by these old people are so obvious that their commitment needs explaining. If your grandmother or mine were to make such a sacrifice on the basis of principle, would we not want to know why? Would you not have expected those who have reported this event to have asked them why? Have you read their answers anywhere? I haven't.

It's the discipline and courtesy extended to all within the confines of this marae that are felt everywhere. Food is cooked continuously by gas fire, in tents with the sides raised and the floors bare. There are no written rosters. People appear and disappear at intervals, yet the work continues unabated. The rain comes and goes without disturbing the rhythm of service the cooks provide the guests. People kiss and embrace regularly. Children are both present and not a bother. The death of the little one in the fountain was obviously a crisis point for these people. What was the message of this fatality? Was it for or against this occupation? These are all matters for discussion, reflection and constant talk. Maori is the language spoken here. I'm astonished that after years of going on marae throughout the North Island, this is my most potent experience of the language being used so extensively by young and old, in formal and informal contact. Spoken English is the exception. There is much speculation about what the council may do, what the police response will be, but there is no fear. That's what is so different here, compared to life on Bastion Point. No endless discussions about whether or not to be arrested. A simple peaceful belief that this issue is right and whatever the price required, it will be paid.

Thursday morning, pre-dawn, and the prayer of the kaumatua in the wharenui begins as it has done, no doubt daily, for years. The chanting of this karakia goes on for a long time. Sleeping with the old men and old women has been very reassuring. The tent leaking drips on my head keeps me up part of the night, but it is a small inconvenience to bear. The question to the front of my mind is a simple one. Does this occupation have merit? Is this claim justified? For Pakeha New Zealanders, these are the important questions. The fact that so many elderly people are present, and prepared to be arrested for their support of this issue, is a powerful affirmation that something serious indeed is happening here, and for the most part, the country is not privy to it.

The day's events show why. And it is not a great start. The gathering media contingent has its first story. A taiaha goes through the window of a car. The violence attracts the media. A road block set up spontaneously by Garden occupants proves provocative, and the inevitable results. The violence is inexcusable and the fact that it happens without mandate from those in control of the marae appears weak in explanation, even if plainly true. Through the day other events attract media attention, such as the agitation outside the Mayor's shop during the march through the town. Moko-wearing Maori make great copy when tension, fear and drama whet the audience's appetite.

But all this attention is largely misdirected. Tensions between angry young Maori and police will remain until the main issues are dealt with. The media frenzy over these one or two acts of violence is a sideshow. Violence of this nature is never acceptable. But nor should it dominate the coverage, especially when the substance of the issues that underpin this occupation is still scarcely understood.

It's now midday and the numbers have swelled well past a thousand. They are all being welcomed, fed and informed. The issues are being debated continuously by each successive group and it is all taking place in Maori. Of the 40 or so media contingent, my checking turns up three or four who speak Maori. In short, the eight hours of discussion taking place on the marae prior to the eviction deadline are being intelligently monitored by less then ten per cent of those whose job it is to tell us what is going on. Rather, media concentration immediately goes to events and activities they understand; the stoush about the car, the abuse during the march, the drunks at the pub. The substance is being missed, time and again, and readers and viewers are left none the wiser.

As the 5pm deadline approaches the count of people gathered has now leapt to two or three thousand, it's hard to say. The number of Pakeha faces multiplies, especially the young people. News of a religiously inspired vigil of townspeople with black armbands silently linking arms around the perimeter receives loud cheers of appreciation from those of us now gathered thickly in front of the meeting house. The music is raucous from Maori performers, the atmosphere one of celebration. As the deadline passes the kuia rise in front of the wharenui and begin to sing and dance. Their waiata is strong, graceful and determined, and the people respond passionately and loudly with soaring spirits. Nowhere in this group of thousands is there any sense of aggravation or threat, yet the hourly IRN news bulletin persists in describing the atmosphere as tense and highly volatile.

We hear the council have changed tack and Paul Holmes in his evening show attacks the Mayor about his 'back-down'. It might have been more useful for Holmes to discover on behalf of the rest of us why the Mayor, in concert with the Assistant Police Commissioner and some iwi representatives, actually considered the deadline was simply the wrong approach. That it wouldn't and couldn't work, and that another strategy was required to break the deadlock and determine the facts. Holmes is so busy trying to get the Mayor to acknowledge his supposed lack of spine that the real story, the story his viewers need to know, passes him by.

I have several questions for the media. What about researching the title of this land and reading and understanding some of the history of the events around the Wanganui purchases, so as to be able to explain this to your predominantly Pakeha audience? What about getting to grips with Maori sovereignty and dissecting tino rangatiratanga? A good start might be to consider whether multiple expressions of this sovereignty already well accepted in daily life have actually disadvantaged non-Maori. Good examples are the kohanga reo movement in preschools and the kura kaupapa Maori in the primary and secondary schooling system. Are non-Maori worse off because of these Maori expressions of self-help development? Has settlement of some claims such as those surrounding Bastion Point enhanced Maori lifestyle and objectives, to the detriment of non-Maori?

The smart media would ask the current custodians of Pakaitore about their plans for the small marae, should ownership be acknowledged in their favour. How would the use that the citizens of Wanganui have made of this park change? Would they still have access, as they have had in the past? In short, good journalism would go right to the heart of the issue to address the basic fears of their audience, and determine if these fears are real or imaginary. This is not happening at Pakaitore.

So the real story remains yet to be told. Readers, listeners and viewers everywhere deserve better from their news media than the meagre diet they have been fed about the drama of Moutoa Gardens. The issues being played out in Wanganui need intelligent discussion and translation. New Zealanders know that the clear and unflinching examination of our past will not be easy, nor will trite solutions suffice. But to reach settlements, the people have to be informed. Journalists have a key job here and, in this instance, they are failing in their brief.

Ten years have passed and things have changed. There have in fact been some steps toward resolution at Pakaitore. Steps that would not have been taken had the people not made their presence felt during the occupation. A good summary of the progress to date comes from the *Maori Law Review* of February 2001. The agreement over the future of the land involves three parties: Wanganui District Council, Atihaunui-a-Paparangi and the Crown. It brings to an end the dispute over this land, which had been vested in the Wanganui District Council in 1880, and which had been occupied by protesters in 1995. The agreement is signed by the Mayor of Wanganui on behalf of the district council, three representatives of Atihaunui-a-Paparangi and the Prime Minister on behalf of the Crown.

The *Law Review* reports:

> The three parties have agreed that the vesting of the reserve area by the Crown should be cancelled by the Minister of Conservation under s27 Reserves Act 1977, with the consent of the District Council. The cancellation will be noted in the Gazette and the land will revert to the Crown, maintaining its historic reserve status. A reserves board will then be established under s30 Reserves Act 1977, consisting of three District Council, three Whanganui iwi and one Crown representatives. This is described as a joint management arrangement. The detailed terms of reference and accountability for the joint Management Board 'will need to be discussed between the three parties'. The board will be obliged to manage the historic reserve under the Reserves Act, which includes granting permission to applicants to use the gardens, and maintaining the public access and use of the area. A damaged statue of John Ballance in the gardens will be repaired and reinstated. Its location may be changed after consultation with the Ballance family and it may be removed to another part of Wanganui. A second sculpture removed during the occupation of the gardens will be replaced and will include a Maori stone carving.

All this was achieved after extensive negotiations between the parties over a long period, leading to a provisional agreement in 2000. This agreement was taken back by the iwi representatives to their own people at a series of initial hui, and approval of the final form of the agreement was gained at final hui in February 2001. The council also approved the agreement by a vote held in an ordinary meeting after a period of public consultation involving 259 submissions. Currently meetings of the joint management board are governed by sections 30–32 of the Reserves Act 1977, which provide that a chairman of the board may be appointed by the Minister of Conservation or may be elected by the board members. The chairman has the casting vote where votes are tied.

Understanding the Maori and Pakeha interface

As successful as this negotiation was, it had not led to the complete dissipation of all tension around these matters. The iwi groupings agreed with the land moving out of council control, but saw its vesting in the Crown as a second-best option next to having title themselves. The council had not had in its plans, prior to negotiations, the joint management of its own facilities with iwi. Nevertheless, the compromise has seen a more mature Treaty arrangement than previously existed. It has drawn Crown, iwi and council in the same structure of kaitiakitanga, exercising explicit guardianship of the land and recognising that joint responsibility calls for the cooperation of all parties.

So why does it take protest and occupation to open us all up to an historical reality that in the twenty-first century ought to be obvious? Michael King's *Penguin History of New Zealand* (of which 100,000 copies have now been sold) is an acute reminder that we all need to be confident in our grasp of our own nationhood and how it has developed. The need to know has become paramount, for without the knowledge and the perspective offered by understanding of the Maori and Pakeha interface over the years issues like Pakaitore are truly unfathomable. It is this knowledge deficit, the lack of the appreciation of the details of our own history, that trips us up time and again.

We are fortunate that such is the state of generally positive alchemy among all New Zealanders of whatever whakapapa origins that we do not live in constant agitation. But it would be a mistake to equate relative silence with acquiescence. The Moutoa Gardens example and the foreshore and seabed hikoi of 2004 show that sharp reminders are waiting in the wings when insufficient attention is paid to getting the relationships right between tangata whenua and tauiwi.

This is not just the case on the Maori side of the equation. In fact, many Pakeha are fed up with the occasional uprising. Often enough such protest is seen as tedious and repetitive, the grounds for agitation spurious or even laughable. It is at this point that most care should be taken not to overstate the case. There are occasions when Maori groups or individuals push the envelope beyond the boundaries of an issue's merits. When this occurs relationships become toxic very quickly. Such was the case with the resource consent issue in Manukau City in 2004, when local hapu representatives claimed wahi tapu status for some private land. The developer went to great expense to deal with the issues that unnecessarily prolonged the granting of the consent, only to discover that the hapu had got the original designation wrong. It does not matter to the general population that there are hundreds of consent applications approved every year where Maori applicants do not succeed with their submissions. One incident where the process trips up, and non-Maori are the injured party, is sufficient to bring the whole Resource Management Act (RMA) into disrepute.

This is an example where the rules are clearly different for Maori than for almost everybody else. One slip-up by Maori, one example of overreaching and commercial avarice at the expense of someone else, and the cultural discrediting resounds. A similar failure by non-Maori and 'That's just business.' No cultural impugning is assumed.

In Aotearoa the democratic dynamic gives default preference to the dominant Pakeha cultural and legal interpretations and practices with respect to acquiring, owning and developing land, air and water rights. Such a dynamic assumes that Maori are required to make a special case if their interests are to be represented. It is, for instance, perfectly appropriate for developers to negotiate the sale of 'air rights' over high-rise buildings in downtown Auckland, but potentially outrageous that Maori owners contemplate charging commercial operators for comparable 'use rights' on the lakes to which they have title. It is acceptable that buildings be designated 'historic' and thus preserved and restricted in their development use because of their significance to our cultural heritage, but distressing and obstructive when Maori designations of sites of significance (such as wahi tapu) prevent unencumbered development. The RMA provides in a structured sense the right for the Maori voice to be heard, without extending to that voice any kind of veto right. It is somewhat sobering that many reformers, agitating around the efficiency and effectiveness of this Act, wish to see the removal of even this basic protection of Maori views and interests. As with many other aspects of the Treaty relationship, a large dose of perspective is helpful. Anxiety over 'special' resource management privileges for Maori does not survive close examination of the evidence. In commercial terms, the greatest threat to developers and their progress comes not from Maori, but from other developers. It is the competition for financial, legal and commercial leverage that feeds most of the agitation in this marketplace.

BHP New Zealand Steel and Ngaati Te Ata at Maioro

Nevertheless, the historical healing that can occur when all parties come to their senses about issues over land, title and ownership is now exemplified by large and small initiatives everywhere in Aotearoa. An important illustration of the value of just such a healing is provided by BHP New Zealand Steel and Ngaati Te Ata over sand mining for the steel mill at Glenbrook in South Auckland.

This had been a matter of significant and persistently angry interchanges between the parties. In effect, Ngaati Te Ata went into occupation in 1990 at Maioro, a location used by the company for mining. The iwi asserted that the sand mines were within their rohe and contained koiwi (human remains) of tupuna, as a result of historical urupa. For several years the company and the iwi battled it out, often in unedifying public confrontation. A circuit breaker was necessary.

A change of management at the mill and a change of attitude by the iwi created the opportunity to advance. With the creative skill of Tahuna Minhinnick on the one hand and the willingness of Mike O'Connell, the mine manager, and Maurice Brighouse, the raw materials manager, on the other, a strategy was agreed. Maurice Brighouse wrote: 'The relationship between BHP and Ngaati Te Ata has not been good for several reasons. I am committed to making amends on behalf of the company by developing an improved relationship with Ngaati Te Ata as tangata whenua.'

The Maioro Koiwi Protection plan was launched with the kaupapa (purpose) of allowing the mining to proceed in line with a comprehensive koiwi protection plan. In addition, both Ngaati Te Ata and the mill undertook to develop a successful longstanding relationship and, while acknowledging their past difficulties, sought to find a positive way to move forward.

BHP NZ Steel is a hard-headed commercial organisation that is respected for its competence. In a company report at the time of the agreement, managing director Jim Howard had this to say:

> BHP New Zealand Steel recognises Ngaati Te Ata as tangata whenua and seeks to build a relationship of strength with this iwi. Internationally BHP is committed to recognising and respecting the importance of culture, heritage and traditional rights of indigenous people. We will have achieved our goal when we have earned a reputation as a trusted and responsible citizen, having developed a sense of community partnership that provides a base of support for our business.

As part of a structure to improve this relationship a representative team from both iwi and the company was developed. The approach adopted at the first discussions was to allow explicitly for both parties to have their goals met. Clearly, both parties had their own imperatives. The company wished to have resource consents extended into the distant future. They wished to continue to extract iron sand for the making of steel. The concern for iwi was care and protection of koiwi. They also wanted to benefit from the sand mine extraction in the future by way of royalty, and they wanted resources for marae activities.

As a starting point the representative group addressed as a first priority a fundamental question related to the working environment: 'Is leaving koiwi where they are the best form of protection for them?' In short, what was to be done about the forces of nature that were so disturbing to existing historical burial sites? They went further than this, to address the kind of learning both the company needed from Ngaati Te Ata and the iwi needed from the company. Ngaati Te Ata offered cultural awareness programmes for the mill staff, marae visits, experience of hangi and schooling in tikanga particular to their tribal group. The company offered in return support for marae employment programmes, job opportunities at Glenbrook and Maioro, scholarship funds for education and health, an environment fund that included sponsorship of an environmental scientist, and support for a medical and dentistry outreach at Tahuna marae.

Eventually agreement was reached about all aspects of the protection of the koiwi, including appropriate protocols when human remains were discovered. The mill has been able to proceed with its mining of iron sands, confident of its future supply of raw material and intelligently schooled in the relationship with the iwi. The company offered a formal apology to Ngaati Te Ata for its historically poor behaviour. Crucially, the iwi agreed to consider the cultural, spiritual and environmental impacts of the resource consents and would seek to reach agreement on supporting these. If there were to be disagreements, such differences would be signalled well in advance in a 'no surprises' manner, and each of the parties would look to protecting their own interests.

This is how Tahuna Minhinnick, the chief negotiator for Ngaati Te Ata, saw it:

> The outcomes achieved from the BHP/Ngaati Te Ata negotiations were a result of choosing a 'we help you/ you help us' course from the outset. What we found was that Ngaati Te Ata had to create new tikanga not to stop development but to allow BHP to continue mining without culturally offending Ngaati Te Ata. The question we had to answer was: how can BHP mine a burial ground? That is one of the most difficult cultural questions we have ever had to consider in my lifetime. We decided to change the question from 'how do you mine a burial ground?' to 'how do we best protect ancestral remains?' Not mining was one way, but was it the best way? We created a way that allowed BHP to mine to its maximum potential. Over thirty years that equates to a ninety billion dollar contribution to the New Zealand economy. The proposed Koiwi Protection Plan met the cultural concerns and interests of Ngaati Te Ata one hundred per cent. The key point is the Resource Management Act had allowed for Ngaati Te Ata and BHP to meet on a level playing field. In the old days NZ Steel would bully, Ngaati Te Ata would occupy. The issues never had a chance to be considered. Ngaati Te Ata would never have considered creating a solution to the mining problems faced by BHP. The 'we help you/you help us' platform that developed through the RMA process was definitely the key ingredient to achieving our desired outcomes. Without the RMA we

would still be knocking heads and BHP, the new tenants, would probably have mothballed the company by now and gone back to Australia. An important thing about developing a good relationship with iwi is you only have to do it once. You have to piss Maori off a whole lot of times to ruin a relationship that's been developed.

Effectively, the arrangements made business partners out of former antagonists. It remains hugely ironic that this was achieved with a major multinational that has its head office in Australia. This large and commercially driven company eventually had the foresight to do both the right and the commercially savvy thing, when so many of our own home-grown corporates can see only risks with few benefits in such a Treaty engagement. Time and again opportunity is lost for both commercial gain and improved relationships because attention is not paid to the foundations of the Treaty relationship. At the steel mill all participants now benefit, and the bitter disputes are a fading memory, with a plainly sensible outcome having been achieved for all.

7 : A Treaty-based approach that works for us all

Health Care Aotearoa and the primary health organisation (PHO) revolution

Adopting a Treaty-based approach to organisational decision-making where it is appropriate ought not to be mysterious or divisive. Consider for a moment if we, as a nation, were to set ourselves a basic benchmark for such an approach, with outcomes that were better than the status quo, and benefits that were available to all. If this were indeed possible, why wouldn't we do more of it? We might, if we knew more about how it worked, much as we now understand the way we vote.

As a community we are skilful at adapting to new forms of social organisation while eschewing recklessness. Within the last ten years we have completely changed our voting system from FPP (first past the post) to MMP (mixed member proportional). The transition has been smooth. The first election under the new system had plenty of drama, as the two main parties courted the crucial third party to gain a political majority. No one panicked as the outcome of the final deliberations was awaited. Over the last decade, an appreciation of the political consequences of the change has begun to emerge. But we have needed all three elections under the new approach to achieve a degree of relaxation about its impact, while still alert to its imperfections. We are wise not to ignore the nuances of the system. MMP has entailed a vastly different experience for the political players than it has for the rest of us. For the first time, the 'winners' are not necessarily in control of all the elements. Those wishing to govern have to negotiate key agreements on issues that have the potential to divide.

On the whole, most things stay the same, but at critical points of difference negotiations are undertaken, and deals are struck. In fact, the majority of New Zealanders feel more comfortable now that there is some fettering of absolute power. Ironically, this need for mutual accommodation is less, not more, inclined to foster extremism.

Health Care Aotearoa

For practitioners of a Treaty-based approach to organisational development, the experience is similar. Incremental processes of adjustment similar to those resulting from the adoption of MMP apply also in the cultural arena, and the results are similar. Such an approach leads to moderation, not extremism; and the outcomes have been good for all New Zealanders, not just Maori.

Let me offer a case in point. For the last decade I have been a business adviser to Health Care Aotearoa (HCA), a not-for-profit grouping of primary health providers. This network comprises fifty-five health providers, mostly general practices, and today it operates a coherent, efficient and fully functioning Treaty-based approach to its governance and management. This has not always been the case.

The seed of this network was sown in Otahuhu in South Auckland. A group of bar staff in the Hotel and Hospital Workers Union challenged their union to do something about their members' poor access to primary health care. The union leadership took up the challenge and approached the Minister of Health, saying they were prepared to set up primary health centres if they could get State support, but the business and operating model would have to change. It would not be business as usual. They gave the minister a proposition that contained five simple ideas. In sum, they wanted the health service to:

- provide team-based primary care, where all staff were salaried and where patients who visited the practice were seen by the health professional most appropriate to deal with them, not always the doctor;
- be not-for-profit;
- deliver affordable, accessible and culturally appropriate care, focused on low-income workers;
- be run with the patients as part of the governance;
- be funded on a different basis from orthodox general practice; most crucially, they wanted the funder to stop paying doctors to see individual patients and start paying the service to look after whole populations of registered patients.

Although this proposition gained ministerial support, it was actively opposed by local doctors on the basis of unfair competition. They said it would provide improved care for only a tiny group of poor patients, while the vast majority of poor patients in their practices would miss out. In the event, the Otahuhu Union Health Service opened with a full staff and almost no patients. Nevertheless, after two years it had reached commercial viability.

Newtown in Wellington was the base for a similar experiment, again backed by the Hotel and Hospital Workers Union. It was led by veteran activist Pat Kelly with John Ryall, a key union organiser, doing the hands-on work. A kaupapa Maori model had been discussed with local runanga but rejected as precipitate; nonetheless, support was offered to the initiative. The emphasis was expanded and the union sponsored a community coalition to take control. Fourteen years on, this service has 8000 patients and an ethnically diverse governing board. It has pioneered the delivery of a comprehensive mental health service at GP level, and operates the most extensive refugee and migrant outreach of any primary care service in the country.

Within five years of the Otahuhu and Newtown initiatives there were six of these union and community services, located in Auckland, Wellington and Christchurch. Their approach was quite different from orthodox general practice. Management actively sought to recruit the full range of health professionals — nurses, midwives, community health workers, doctors and health educators — who stood for the same vision, a transformation in primary care. Quite simply, they encouraged staff to think and act in ways that would improve primary health provision for the marginalised. Staff who chose to join these services needed to be committed to this purpose. Pivotal to this was research. The drive was to use the available evidence to press for improved access to primary health care for people on low incomes. Where the evidence to help explain health inequalities was missing, the requirement was to set up projects to research and find it.

By 1993 the market-driven health reforms based on the implementation of the Gibbs Report ('Unshackling the Hospitals') were underway, and the unions decided the most effective means of improving access for low-income patients was to form coalitions. One of the outcomes of the reforms had been a growing opportunity for Maori to set up health provision for themselves. The mantra of 'choice' in service served Maori development aspirations well. So there were emerging a few Maori providers with whom to talk about some form of alliance. In the event the strategy succeeded, with the union services coalescing with Maori, Pacific and community not-for-profit organisations to represent the interests of those with the greatest difficulty in accessing affordable, quality care. The coalition named their network Health Care Aotearoa Inc. (HCA), and its provider members now service over 150,000 low-income New Zealanders.

The advent of Primary Health Organisations (PHOs)

A decade later this initiative has spawned a huge change in primary health care as the government implements its policy of Primary Health Organisations (PHOs), predicated on a way of targeting health funding called the deprivation index. This index grew from research overseen by Peter Crampton and Clare Salmond from the Wellington School of Medicine, and built on work by an epidemiologist, Judy Reinken. Peter Crampton, a public health specialist, was one of the first doctors employed by the Porirua Union and Community Health Centre. This centre was an original HCA member, along with Hauora Hokianga, of which Judy Reinken was a foundation board member. PHOs have other features similar to HCA. They are not-for-profit, have community representation on their governance structures, are funded on a population basis, provide low fees for high-needs patients and have Treaty-based relationships in their governance. The insistence that the people being served must have a say in the policy by which the PHO functions originated from this group's core philosophy.

Once again, as if an echo from 1987, the doctor provider groups initially opposed this move. They claimed it provided improved care for only a tiny group of poor patients, while the vast majority of poor patients in their practices missed out. They also objected to community participation in their governance. In fact, this objection was never sustainable. The take-up by the general practitioners themselves told a different story. By the end of 2004, over 75 per cent of New Zealanders were successfully enrolled with PHOs and over half of all New Zealanders have seen a decrease in their primary health costs at the doctor and the chemist.

A Treaty-based process

While this is a good example of a grass-roots initiative informing national policy and benefiting the lives of over half of all New Zealanders, it would not have occurred had it not been for a quite explicit application of a Treaty-based process. The conceptual framework HCA developed to guide its provision of care to Maori, Pacific and low-income people came through a policy of cultural inclusion. The metaphor for that inclusion is the Treaty. But such a sophisticated understanding was not immediately present in the early days of its development. It needed time to emerge.

In the first stages of its constitution this loose-knit coalition of virtual strangers struck common ground mostly in their commitment to improving the health of the population they wished to service, not on the basis of a joint commitment to Treaty principles. A meeting was held in Wellington in early 1994 to confirm the decision to form a network organisation.

HCA members had to be not-for-profit, community-governed or iwi/hapu organisations that emphasised the provision of services to low-income populations. The members wanted to be totally transparent in their approach to spending government health money, hence the willingness to share all financial information with the State at a provider level. No other medical provider grouping was prepared to do this. This was ground-breaking stuff. There were no comparable primary care networks to serve as models, except for the independent provider associations (IPAs) owned by doctor collectives and managed as profitable enterprises.

What was special about HCA was the quality and vision from within those initial provider groups. But still in that first meeting in 1994 the focus was not on the Treaty, although a founding member of the network was Te Oranganui Iwi Health Authority, the parent body of Te Waipuna Health Centre, a kaupapa Maori primary health service based in

Wanganui. The Authority was chaired by Niko Tangaroa and had as its CEO Tariana Turia. Both these people were formative in developing a Treaty-based approach, and the catalyst for this was the first HCA national hui, held that same year on Tariana's home marae at Whangaehu near Wanganui.

Newly minted this diverse clutch of HCA members may have been, but they were not inexperienced in their field. They were leaders from union organisations, political organisations, community groups and public health organisations. They had well-developed political antennae, personal stature and considerable collective clout. They were also overwhelmingly Pakeha. But at this inaugural hui a strong, resolute and intellectually expansive challenge awaited.

Tariana Turia was invited to present her perspective on health from the standpoint of leading a kaupapa Maori health service. She responded by providing a simple, eloquent and clear account of the elements that constituted good health for Maori. This traversed her personal experience and that of her husband, George. She covered the tribal history of her hapu and the life experience of being Maori in that small community. It was a spell-binding first-hand account of the world as seen through the eyes of Maori, not as victim, nor as a social drain on the State, but as one person's story that was representative of a people determined not to relinquish their own authenticity as tangata whenua. It was about health, but not as we knew it.

Pivotal to her explanation were two inescapable truths. There would be no health for Maori without recovery of their whenua and recognition of their rangatiratanga. This was such a different philosophical approach from that of the mainstream health providers that it provided a profound challenge to network members. In Tariana's world, health meant a commitment to the Treaty because inherent in this process was an affirmation of Maori recovery of self — in short, control over their own affairs. 'Give us what is due to us, and we will deliver the service to our own people.'

If HCA was to be serious about addressing the determinants of Maori ill-health, it needed first to decide its own position on the Treaty. Where did it stand on the issue of affirming and protecting te tino rangatiratanga? Even given the vast experience of the people present, not all were equally equipped to face this challenge. While many had Treaty workshop training and had done some revisiting of our nation's history, there was still a kind of Pakeha awkwardness over the subject of rangatiratanga. For most, it still represented unfamiliar territory. Faced with the eloquence of Tariana on the one hand, and the embracing knowledge of the tikanga appropriate to HCA from Niko Tangaroa, Joe Topia and Chris Diamond (the latter two both kaumatua of Hauora Hokianga) on the other, this challenge was beginning to look more than formidable to the tauiwi members of the network. The Maori partners, though initially small in numbers, appeared substantially more competent in an all-round, fully integrated sense than their Pakeha counterparts.

Fortunately the Pakeha leadership, following the example of the first coordinator for the network, Peter Glensor, picked up the take (issue). Peter was manager of a small but significant health service in Pomare, Lower Hutt. In the formative days of HCA he spent just part of his time as a coordinator for the network. His service was located in a community house in one of the highest needs areas in the district; from the beginning it had taken a whole-of-life approach to health provision. People came to the service not just to see health professionals, but because there were weaving, budgeting and cooking classes. There was also an informal food bank and a preschool play group. Your child might see a children's health nurse and you could ask for help to sit for your driver's licence. While initially light on funds, the service was very strong on innovation. The centre also had a very high number of Maori and Pacific patients on its register.

Peter's leadership was important to the intellectual focusing of the network, but he was not alone. Bridget Allan, who was the CEO of Hauora Hokianga, a major independent health provider in the Far North, had been elected the network's first chairperson. As a Pakeha living and working in a majority Maori context, her cultural reflexes had been trained by the ordinary activities of everyday life. Hauora Hokianga was community owned and operated, but was not regarded by Maori as a kaupapa Maori service, because ownership did not reside with iwi or hapu. Bridget was thus used to the ambiguities of leading a service that served a dominant Maori population with an organisation that was not uniformly recognised by consumers and stakeholders as Maori-focused, even if it was patently Maori-friendly.

Peter Glensor had been a founding partner in the Waitangi Consultancy, a commercial partnership that provided practical Treaty support for both government and non-government organisations wanting to address their structures and behaviours. This was one Pakeha with a comprehensive view of both our Maori and our Pakeha history, and he was to become a clever organiser and advocate for the members of the network. He brought with him one other advantage — a moderate working familiarity with te reo Maori. Together, Peter and Bridget did more than most to facilitate the framing of the tauiwi response to the take laid down by Tariana, a response that has the network fully bicultural today.

Essentially Peter encouraged an explicit recognition in the network's constitution of the status of tangata whenua as the first people of Aotearoa and one of the joint founding parties to the Treaty, the Crown and tauiwi being the other. This understanding found its eventual form in the constitutional rules of the network that allowed for no fewer than 50 per cent of the executive to be from Maori organisations, and for a rotating chair and deputy chair of Maori/tauiwi selected on the same basis. Currently the chair is Alayna Watene, CEO of Te Taiwhenua o Heretaunga health services in Hawke's Bay.

From the beginning there has been a discouragement of any form of tokenism. HCA was not going to get away with anything less than a full examination of the relationships between Treaty partners. Ngati Porou from the East Coast of the North Island were going to see to that. Not long after the network was formed, they arrived at the annual hui in large numbers to investigate an invitation to membership. This was a testing experience for both parties. Ngati Porou Hauora wished to assess whether this predominantly Pakeha network (to date) had the capacity to look at the underlying reasons for Maori health deprivation and to advocate the kind of measures that would address these real causes. Existing network members wanted to assess whether, along with the urgency and intellectual acumen that the iwi brought to their analysis, they had the capacity for including non-Maori players. This mating dance took the best part of a year, before Ngati Porou applied for full membership and the network unanimously approved their acceptance.

The network quickly developed its own unique organisational behaviours. An example has been the management of discussion at both the annual general meeting and at the annual national hui. The network runs its affairs with two caucuses — tangata whenua and tauiwi. Within the tauiwi caucus are Pakeha and Pacific sub-caucuses. For those not used to this style of discussion and decision-making, this can sometimes be an intimidating or inhibiting experience. However, it doesn't take long to get over the initial discomfort and reluctance to participate. Over a three-day hui the separate caucus approach may be used for three or four hours. The balance of time is spent with all participants together in full session or in open workshops. It is not unusual for these hui to have 150–200 people present from the member organisations' medical, nursing and administrative staff, governance and patient population.

In quite pragmatic ways, the network thus embraces the Treaty and affirms protection for the rangatiratanga of tangata whenua. It also affirms the authentic standing and legitimacy of tauiwi deriving from that same Treaty. From this base it gains licence to address matters of health outcomes from a much wider perspective than just the medical intervention strategies. This wider perspective offers a whole-of-life view of health that can be understood just as easily by Pakeha as by Maori, even if the language of description is different.

Community engagement — a vital ingredient

HCA regards community engagement as a key pillar for health transformation for low-income people. There has to be a creative and genuine counterweight to the solely medical practitioner groups in health care. The context for this counterweight is the community development approach that sees the presenting health symptoms of disadvantaged people not simply in terms of medical diagnosis but in relation to their housing, employment and the state of their personal relationships. For this approach to work it must reach the groups that are hardest to engage, often providing health promotion programmes along with curative services. Provision of care for the middle classes is not the central tenet of this philosophy, although all New Zealanders stand to benefit as no one is turned away.

The value of this wider approach was supported by George Salmond, former Director-General of Health and an early individual member of the network. George saw in this network legitimisation of a wider vision of the role of primary care in health communities. The network therefore took as its template the 1979 Alma Ata Declaration of the World Health Organization, which relates to people's rights to health care. Don Matheson and Julia Carr, both Pakeha, became two of the most articulate supporters of the application of this template to the New Zealand context. Not long back from Zimbabwe, where they had worked as GPs in the rural heartland after independence, they were part of the initiating group and became employed as the first two GPs with the Newtown Union Health Service. In 1995 they moved to the East Coast and Don became first the hospital manager for Te Puia, then the general manager of Ngati Porou Hauora. Julia became the clinical leader of mental health services. Ngati Porou had Te Puia Hospital within its rohe but it was being run and administered by the Gisborne Crown Health Enterprise (CHE). At that stage Ngati Porou had little control over any of the services on the Coast, which was a source of significant irritation for the iwi — a negative reflection on their mana. Not only were they not in control of an asset that was right in the middle of the East Coast; they had to fend off almost continuous plans and strategies geared to its imminent closure. For Ngati Porou the hospital was a taonga, an iconic health opportunity — if only they could get their hands on it. Their instruction to Don Matheson was to get it back!

An opportunity to press the case arose when Ngati Porou hosted the annual HCA hui in 1997 and nearly 200 people descended on Tokomaru Bay for three days of conference. Guest of honour was Bill English — or 'Wiremu Pakeha', as he was christened in the powhiri. The National Party had not been seen as a natural ally by the network, but this Minister of Health had a relaxed capacity to be himself in that strongly Maori milieu with a very diverse audience. Don Matheson, Peter Glensor, Bridget Allan and I had a conversation with him at a break in one of the sessions. We pushed the case hard for recognition of the capacity of Ngati Porou Hauora (then still in its early development years) to take over the hospital and to be bulk-funded for delivery of all the health care on the Coast. The CHE had been resolutely opposed to devolving its responsibility, preferring to control the region and the resources related to service delivery from Gisborne.

The matter was a controversial one. The subtext was about trust — the kind of trust required to transfer the management of considerable turnover and assets to a Maori organisation and away from a Crown entity. The unspoken apprehension: could Maori be trusted to run it well? The role of the network staff within our Treaty-based strategy was to demonstrate the sound case for the transfer by our advocacy and clear grasp of the questions at issue. In short, there was a broker role to be played here, Pakeha to Pakeha, to support the Maori kaupapa. This was not a question of speaking for Ngati Porou; they were their own best advocates. This was a process of speaking in support of their position in a manner that could be seen as having merit in Pakeha terms.

It is this kind of nuance that has so often tripped people up in their attempts at Treaty processes. In particular, it is the Pakeha's fear of being cast as someone who usurps the role of the tangata whenua, speaking for them and thus diminishing their own representation of their own affairs. This is a genuine anxiety, but one that can easily be addressed. The practice adopted by HCA staff was one of continuous consultation with our members. Almost always, a clear consensus was reached on how to proceed. Sometimes mistakes were made and these were noted, often in very public contexts, but this was only sound training. Like any skill, cross-cultural advocacy requires knowledge, and training is often necessary. But this is the case for most things of value in life. New Zealand business people are recognised as some of the most entrepreneurial in the world, able to trade anywhere and to learn the nuances required to be successful. Typically, however, we have been less interested in understanding the cross-cultural requirements within our own country. The derision accorded to the 'politically correct' stance is the default mechanism for doing nothing, when in fact so much more progress is made when there is a real effort to understand. Bill English understood this.

For the iwi, vindication was close at hand. The minister made the decision in their favour, enabling them to take over the provision of health care in 1999, and today Ngati Porou control nearly all health service delivery on the Coast, including Te Puia Hospital. The service has expanded, with the equivalent of over 130 full-time staff providing a complete range of primary and low-level secondary services. Equity in their balance sheet has grown more than three-fold, and unlike most of the District Health Boards in the country their operating accounts have been in aggregate operating surplus for the last five years. Re-invigoration of iwi rangatiratanga, stimulated by the transfer of assets and control of health provision, has not only proved to be sound stewardship, but all the people on the Coast — Maori and Pakeha alike — have access to better health services. So successful has this transition been that the current board, led by CEO Dianne Gibson, has opened a new general practice in Kaiti, the southernmost part of their rohe within Gisborne. It experienced financial difficulties in the first two years but is now a thriving and growing health service, open to all residents of the area.

HCA can claim modest success as a Treaty-based organisation that not only manages to enhance the capacity of its membership to do its business, but promotes results that benefit all New Zealanders. The advocacy of this group of primary health organisations (PHO) has improved the access to health care of low-income New Zealanders regardless of ethnicity, but without the commitment to a Treaty-based process this would not have occurred. The Maori dimension, fully enfranchised and engaged with the non-Maori dimension, has created the changes in practice and increase in understanding that have charted a pathway to success.

This begs the question of why such alliances are not formed in other parts of our national life where we struggle to reconcile an intuitive, almost archetypal perception of ourselves as a fair, inclusive and just nation of people — with appalling outcomes for some of our citizens in crime, educational achievement, family cohesion and economic advancement. The dilemma is stark. Our bountiful and well-resourced nation nevertheless has an underclass, exposing a cultural deficit that many of us find inexplicable, incomprehensible and contradictory to a coherent sense of nationhood.

Another approach needs to be explored.

If we were to set ourselves a basic benchmark that the outcomes of such an approach should be better than the status quo, and the benefits available to all, then harnessing the inclusive potential of a Treaty-based strategy would end up being positive for all of us. The HCA experience suggests this is not only possible, it is soundly pragmatic.

8 : Reconciling ownership and mana

Speaking past each other on the foreshore

A beach on the Coromandel Peninsula is justifiably famous — for its hot water. There is a period, two hours either side of low tide, when you can dig a hole in one part of the sand and let in the hot flow, or dig in another part to temper it with a cold flow, then bathe or simply bask in this superb natural phenomenon. For whole periods during the day the beach is deserted. Then all of a sudden it is an international cultural muddle, as people from all over the world descend to create, for a brief period, an instant community of accidental intimacy.

Hot Water Beach was where our family stayed briefly with friends for New Year 2005, and I got a real jolt to my thinking. Outside around the evening fire, with the stars so clear, uncluttered by urban lights in a way unfamiliar to us city-dwellers, the conversation turned to the beaches. Who owned them? Who had the right to claim them? And just how was it possible to accommodate both deeply felt *personal* connections on our Pakeha side with different and less well understood *collective* connections on our Maori side? What did all this have to do with the Treaty anyway?

They were obvious questions, but it took the lubricated atmosphere of a balmy summer evening for me to see them so clearly in my head. So I thought I would try for some answers, to make sense of why it might be that the two sides see things so differently, and to examine how close the new foreshore and seabed law came to an answer that would get it right for all New Zealanders. In a phrase, did we solve the dilemma?

A personal starting point was needed. We each have our own stories. But we also need to understand the intention of the new law. Both were critical to unravelling the puzzle. To simply stay with the personal was not going to answer the question satisfactorily.

Every year since 1923, the Snedden family has packed up and headed for the beach over Christmas and New Year. It is a ritual that began with my grandparents in the years of recovery after the First World War, the initial excursions by ferry to Devonport and Takapuna, well before the existence of the Auckland Harbour Bridge. My family never missed a holiday at Takapuna during the whole of my youth, save for one year in which we went to Gisborne when the house we traditionally rented was unavailable. Life at the beach looms large in my life as the earliest image of inclusive and sustained family fun. Dad was on holiday for four weeks, our house at Mt Eden was often lent to friends, and living one street back from the beach was whatever we made of it. The options were endless, with television nowhere to be seen. It was a time of long nights, irregular days, and hospitality to visitors and extended family as our cousins, the Molloys, the family of my father's sister, took up residence next door.

The relaxed nature of this existence is still embedded deeply in my psyche because of its simplicity and its joy. Surprisingly, neither my siblings nor I were surfers. We were moderate swimmers and enthusiastic harvesters of shellfish, most notably pipi, but water sports like water-skiing, yachting and sailing were not our passion. Rugby and cricket occupied our waking moments. Looking back, none of us ever remember the wet summers. It was a blessed time and there were no family tragedies at the beach. As we grew up, the foreshore and seabed was the natural host to our teenage coming-of-age rituals. Walks and fires on the beach, parties and late-night swims, young courtships — both successful and abysmally and embarrassingly tragic — litter my early recollections. It embraced us all.

Finally the draw of the sea proved irresistible to my parents and, in my last year of school, they sold the family home and moved for the last time to Takapuna, just up from the beach. They relished the healing provided in the last years of their lives while they could still walk on the beach. On the sand, with backs to the housing, it was easy to lose yourself in the grandeur of the harbour. Rangitoto, a recently active volcano, emerged on the near horizon, magnificent and immovable. Close enough to imprint itself on the mind's eye yet with sufficient distance to be immutable to the threats of development, it has steadfastly resisted any commercialisation. I am sure my parents found reassurance in this unchanging vista, the island's feet washed by the ebb and flow of the tide, and their own need for spiritual sustenance nourished by the beach as they slowly succumbed to the decline of their bodies. In retrospect I suspect the family shifted to Takapuna because of my parents' sense of impending vulnerability. They intuitively sought out the environment that gave them most joy, and the beach won. No contest.

Those early days were marked by the ordinariness of sharing in this magnificent resource. There were no flash houses on the foreshore then. The drama in the landscape came from the flourishing pohutukawa trees that hung with a kind of impossible majesty from the cliff faces and announced the arrival of summer, as if providing formal consent to down tools and let the relaxation commence. Any commercial advantage of living just off the beachfront was not yet evident. What was clear and deeply felt was that this was a part of the country that was available to all of us, without favour and without question. The only regulation was to swim between the flags, and that was a recent innovation.

Frank Sargeson lived on Esmonde Road, the conduit off the bridge. A right turn past his place and you were on the road to Devonport. Turn left and within a short distance Takapuna township appeared. I was not aware of Sargeson's presence in my youth. Now, more conscious of his importance as a distinctively New Zealand writer and his early mentoring of the talented and now-famous, it is no surprise that the physicality of this island nation and its coastlines features so prominently in our Pakeha literature.

There are the dimensions of pioneer freedom in all of this, the need for simplicity, for getting along with one another and for the self-reliance so familiar to those making their living off sea or land. The classic statement of this was the bach or crib. If anything signalled our singular, untouchable, unregulated sense of self as Pakeha, this was it. At the bach the rules changed, the ambience becoming more primitive, uncluttered. The demands of the 'other life' became temporarily suspended, and time and order played no part save for the requiting of hunger and the maintenance of shelter. Skill at living off the coastline was an artform most admired.

In so many respects, the foreshore provided for many of us Pakeha a powerful and fundamental cultural metaphor of transition. It is the in-between space that can be both land and sea, but for a time neither land nor sea. Our beach life became our in-between life, our moment to be culturally tidal.

That in-between life as beach person is thus one of our most significant Pakeha cultural archetypes. It is archetypal because it goes to the very heart of our identity, so intuitively understood. Few words are required to explain it. While it may remain unarticulated for long periods, its resonance resounds when it is under threat. In 2004, as the debate around the ownership of the foreshore took hold, many Pakeha responded quite viscerally to the threat to public ownership of the beaches. As much as this was a taonga to Maori, something to be protected in respect of their rangatiratanga, so too was it an issue that put our Pakeha cultural identity under immediate threat. The response was widespread alarm and vigorous defence of 'our' coastline. In the resulting ferment the technical definitions of what constituted foreshore (the wet land between mean high-water mark and low tide) and seabed (everything on the 'wet' side of the foreshore) became immaterial.

Here a real contest of cultural values seemed destined for a legislative shoot-out, perhaps with only one winner. Was this inevitable? What was it that Maori were talking about?

Two different approaches — the personal and the collective

I had long been a friend of Grant Hawke. Together with his brother Joe, Grant was active in the occupation of Bastion Point and I had held many discussions with him about the different way Maori approach matters of land and sea. Grant had witnessed the devastating effect the raw sewage outflow had had on Ngati Whatua's harbour and kai moana (seafood) at Okahu Bay. One day we talked about the members of his whanau who had contracted typhoid and died from the infected kai. He had survived the disease but it had him hospitalised for a long period. Grant is now in his sixties, white-haired and with an engaging and gentle manner. With the return of his whenua (Bastion Point) in 1991, he has taken part in the re-invigoration of Ngati Whatua's fortunes.

Get Grant talking on the subject of kaitiakitanga (guardianship) of the harbour and he will astonish with his knowledge of the Waitemata dating to well before the Treaty. What he is referring to are the tribal stories, the naming of aspects of land and harbour, of currents and tides and rocks and fish. The associations he makes relate to the planting and fishing cycles of his own people in this area dating back to the eighteenth century — the kind of stories that Apihai Te Kawau, Ngati Whatua paramount chief in 1840, relayed to Judge Fenton in the Native Land Court of 1868 and which were comprehensively recorded.

These are the cultural practices of a hugely self-sufficient people schooled in the maramataka (Maori calendar) that took its lead not from the days of the year, but the natural cycles of moon and seasons. They had operated an effective and well-proven approach to life on the land and sea, and woven into their life was a system of meaning vital to themselves but, as they discovered, often irrelevant to others. This always vexed Grant Hawke.

> When I see the pollution of our harbours today, when I see our shellfish beds now completely eroded by land reclamation without my people's consent, and our inshore fishing disappear, what should I think? Should I say this is the price of progress? Is this what a sophisticated and civilising society has to offer? I don't think so. Isn't it strange that we are all prepared to live with such a failure in our protection of our harbours and our sea life, in fact much of our taonga (sacred treasures), yet we think that to consider another cultural approach to this is just too hard. Not worth the candle. In fact, more than that. Time after time, we pass laws that make it impossible to take this alternative approach. And people see the resource disappear, and call it progress.

From Grant Hawke's perspective the new Bill was just

another opportunity lost, and while it was especially Maori who were being disadvantaged in the first instance, in fact we were all losing. Grant explained:

> Our tribal history of connection with land and sea is just that, tribal. We are interested in the collective needs of the people. When someone wants something for their own benefit, that's fair enough — but only in a very limited sense. You cannot claim mana over resources such as land and sea (manawhenua, mana moana) unless you agree that these are to be managed for the group. So when the government says to me in the law 'you *personally* can't do this' or 'you can't do that', then I will listen as any New Zealander listens. But when it says to my hapu or my iwi in the way this law is framed, 'you can't apply this thinking' or 'you can't adopt this behaviour' because it's different from the way Pakeha think or behave, then I will object. But I am not objecting just for myself. I am objecting for my group. When we signed the Treaty, the Crown agreed that it would see to the protection of our rangatiratanga. I think that meant that the Crown agreed to protect the way we had acted as *collective* trustees over these things. But not just for ourselves. When Pakeha came, who do they think they relied on to keep them alive? Who gave them the first land to get Auckland started?

In Grant's mind, the Bill was enshrining further that there was only 'one way' of doing things. Its provisions were designed to deal with personal rights. In some areas it explicitly excluded collective perspectives or values that were fundamental to Maori. What's more, as Grant said,

'The evidence everywhere is that the "one way" approach was failing us all.'

How widespread among Maori was Grant's view? A good place to start was with the Waitangi Tribunal, which had convened in January 2004 to receive detailed submissions from both Maori and the Crown over the Bill. Its report contained a rich vein of Maori lore and explanation as iwi from every part of the country spoke about their own specific ties with the coastline, rivers, lakes and harbours within their rohe. At the heart of the issue Maori feared that the Crown's new law would not protect 'te tino rangatiratanga', their capacity to exercise chiefly authority in the way of trusteeship over their taonga and resources. This had been guaranteed under Article 2 of the Treaty. Clearly the foreshore and seabed were part of that treasure.

Article 1 of the Treaty had established a common law and governance (via Parliament, for Maori and non-Maori) and Article 3 had guaranteed to both Maori and settler (new migrants) alike the common right of citizenship. But the chiefs agreed to Article 1 and Article 3 only because of the benefits of the trade-off coming from Article 2, the commitment by the Crown to protect Maori in the exercise of their rangatiratanga. Without the protection of this trade-off, the chiefs would never have agreed to a new system of law or consented to widespread migration and common citizenship. They were in total control and it was precisely by exercising their rangatiratanga that the chiefs gave their authority to the process and signed up. Without this consent, there would have been no deal.

Thus the new law on the foreshore risked further denial and thus diminution of their rangatiratanga and they wanted to stop it. The risk that agitated was that the Crown would once again fail to act to protect the collective rights represented by rangatiratanga.

The Crown also had another problem because it was the Article 2 issues which so often irritated Pakeha, precisely because rangatiratanga related to the collective (tribal structure), not to individuals. But the balance of interests in the proposed law seemed to lean against Maori. The legislation was saying, in effect, as Maori you can have the same rights as all other individual New Zealanders, but you won't have recognised in the way you wish collective rights which, you claim, are guaranteed under Article 2.

Not surprisingly, this dialogue was challenging for lawmakers. What would a 'one law for all' strategy do with Maori philosophy and customary practices pre-1840, practices at the heart of the exercise of rangatiratanga? Could a new law cope with the underlying recognition of whakapapa links to land and sea based on traditional names? How would it deal with the notion that it is all land (whenua), be it wet or dry? Should these pre-1840 practices have the status of territorial customary rights and be taken seriously along with all their associated interests and obligations? Might these rights today in some circumstances amount to outright ownership rights that could be bought and sold, or at the very least, attract a price for use such as through leases?

Lost in all this complex contest was a central truth, little emphasised. Any granting of Maori territorial rights and interests carried with it obligations. There could be no exercise of rights of any sort related to mana without the requisite responsibilities of manaakitanga (hospitality or obligation to the other). In short, the recognition of a right for Maori on the one hand would have been expected to lead to a negotiated reciprocal quid pro quo for the Crown on the other. Unfortunately such a common-sense proposition hardly saw the light of day. The debate was so focused on what rights each might 'lose' that it failed crucially to ask what each of the parties might have agreed to do to honour their reciprocal obligations, had they 'won'. There was also more trouble ahead if this new law was to comprehensively include the Maori cultural dimension. Such a step would require a rethink of our system of lawmaking, seen by many Maori as relentlessly monocultural at its very essence. If Maori were to succeed, this might lead to concessions on 'use rights' or even 'property rights'. These concessions would be based on 'collective' rights different from those customarily derived from our own British legal and historical tradition, based on 'personal' or 'individual' rights. In the event, this conceptual challenge proved politically too difficult. The Pakeha counter-attack shaped up as too strong.

Expressing Pakehatanga

In retrospect, this forceful articulation of Pakehatanga may have taken many Maori by surprise. A dominant culture normally assumes that it operates with power and control and that its own way of doing things is the only or best way. It just gets on with the job, without need for explanation. Its cultural assumptions are mostly covert, operating within the implicit rules understood as acceptable behaviour. Where it spends its 'cultural' time is in determining why other ways of working simply won't fit, or in finding another way of operating without offence to its own mode — the kind of thing that happens when a Crown Minister says we are prepared to have powhiri, but only if they are not too long!

But in this case, the debate explicitly articulated Pakehatanga, or the Pakeha way of conducting our business, in direct contrast to that of Maori cultural practice. Rarely in our history have we as Pakeha described why we feel how we feel, why we behave how we behave, why we say what we say, why we believe what we believe, and thus why we wish to protect what is dear to us. Paradoxically, many Maori might normally have felt completely comfortable with our asserting some of the basis of our own identity. It mirrored in many respects their own cultural reflex. But the race debate that occurred in 2004 following Dr Brash's speech at Orewa meant that these were anything but normal times. For a brief period we experienced as a nation the opportunity for a breakthrough in our cross-cultural relationships. Had we followed through this clarity in cultural assertion of identity and beliefs, it might have sparked a truly mature and inclusive Treaty-based debate. A debate focused on reaching a more sophisticated level of cultural accommodation.

But the opportunity went begging. Why did this happen? Perhaps we were not sufficiently aware of the background to the context that had sparked this conversation in the first place. Some of the answers lay with our recent history.

At one level I am sure my own family's affection for the beach at Takapuna was not untypical of many of us up to the end of the 1970s. As New Zealanders, in our rare moments of public reflection, we would not talk of ourselves and where we came from without reference somewhere in our personal story to our profound, God-given attachment to our land, and most affectionately to our beaches. There was never a price to be put on this, because it was not seen as a commodity to be traded.

But by the next decade two influences had begun to alter this psychological and territorial landscape. The deregulation of the New Zealand economy under the 1984 Labour administration led by David Lange removed the economic constraints that had fettered New Zealand commerce. For better or worse, the entrepreneurs were set free to fly, and to take responsibility for their own crash if it came. The financial markets rose to the prospect of wealth through property speculation. In our own familiar patch the harbour bridge had been opened in 1959 and extended ten years later, crossing the Waitemata to link the North Shore to the city centre and thus making access to Takapuna easy. What formerly constituted a major expedition had become a daily commuter journey. As this kind of easy and quick access to the foreshore became more possible in many parts of New Zealand, so the value of property on the beachfront became attractive as an investment to the financially adventurous.

At the same time Maori leaders were describing loudly and assertively their losses, both cultural and commercial, and pinpointing accurately the Crown's comprehensive failure to acknowledge and protect their rangatiratanga. Included in this failure was the Crown's historical unwillingness to protect sea and waterways and other taonga. Therefore the Lange/Douglas Government's privatisation of State assets presented a clear threat to any Maori keen to advance their interests through the Waitangi Tribunal.

But Lange's Labour Government had also in 1985 authorised the Tribunal to examine grievances back to 1840. This was an important catalyst. Maori were shrewd enough to recognise that if the State-assets sale process was not slowed or subject to Treaty caveat of some sort, the ability of the State to re-enfranchise Maori economically in the future would fast diminish. The Tribunal provided an unprecedented forum to advance their cause. The issues of public ownership or privatisation were now on the agenda. In reality it was Maori who by pursuing their own interests had led the charge to retain State assets in public ownership when most others stood by helplessly. This gave the whole process of the sale of State assets serious cause for pause.

The Crown response

Just as Maori were mobilising, so too successive governments were moving to refine their responses to Tribunal outcomes. Decision after decision had demonstrated a systematic and quite radical historical destruction of Maori rights and possessions by successive government action since 1840. So the Crown continued to evolve and adapt its own position in response. One tactic adopted by the Crown was to stop trying to defend itself in new claims on matters already proven in previous claims. As the evidence piled up — mostly, as with the Ngai Tahu claim, using the Crown's own records — Maori were able to prove deliberate breaches of solemn undertakings in the confiscation of their resources. So Crown officials changed tack from mounting a vigorous defence of the Crown's own actions to focusing their energy on quantifying and restricting the economic damage to the nation. In so doing successive governments restricted the political damage associated with reaching agreement with claimants. The introduction of the Fiscal Envelope policy, designed to limit financial damage by 'capping' the total amount of claims, was an example of this.

Yet Maori enthusiastically took the opportunity to register claims, knowing that the process might well take years. After 150 years of waiting, another decade or two seemed a relatively small cross to bear if that was what it took to get matters resolved.

The period from 1985 to the turn of the millennium was significant for Maori. The Tainui and Ngai Tahu settlements were in effect to be used as benchmark claims for redress against which all others would be assessed. Both these settlements took political nerve on the part of both Crown and claimants. Neither constituency was universally happy. In Pakeha minds both tribal groups were seen as major beneficiaries of Treaty largesse, with financial settlements in advance of $170 million each. In Maori minds the redress was but a minuscule response to the scale of the destitution and destruction to their tribal endowment since 1840.

Not before time, in 1987 te reo Maori was recognised as an official language of New Zealand, and soon after Maori radio broadcasting became a reality. Eventually Maori television was to follow. Maori were also getting traction in the contest with the Crown over the sale of State coal interests. In 1989 the Tainui Maori Trust Board argued that the sale of Coalcorp mines in Huntly would prejudice the ability of Tainui to have access to compensation, should they be successful in their claim before the Tribunal. In a landmark ruling Court of Appeal President Robin Cooke stated that the five judges had reached two overall conclusions. Firstly, that the principles of the Treaty of Waitangi override everything else in the State Owned Enterprises Act, and secondly, that those principles require that Pakeha and Maori Treaty partners act towards each other reasonably and with the utmost good faith.

There was another major advance for Maori in the 1992 Sealord deal and fisheries settlement. The Crown negotiated the purchase of 20 per cent of the existing quota and 27 per cent of new species quota and transferred it to Maori interests. It took a further twelve years for Maori to agree tribally as to how that resource should be shared, and by then its scale had grown to substantial proportions.

In short, as this brief scattering of examples reveals, the fifteen years leading up to 2000 showed mounting evidence of a Maori renaissance. On the foreshore, the emergence of the technology for sophisticated aquaculture farming was requiring new legal frameworks for commercial exploitation. Maori with historical manawhenua links to parts of the coastal marine areas saw chances for commercial risk and gain. In different parts of the country, through joint ventures or on their own account, they were making commercial headway.

Unhappily this was not the experience of tribal groups in the upper South Island. Numerous attempts had been made to seek resource consent for commercial aquaculture farming from the Marlborough District and Regional Councils; while other groups, non-Maori, had been the beneficiaries of such a commercial advantage, all Maori approaches had failed.

As a consequence, and after six fruitless years of trying, a tribal alliance of eight iwi from the top of the South Island, desperate to obtain some negotiating leverage, finally took their case to the Maori Land Court seeking an order declaring land below the high water mark as Maori customary land. They argued that ownership rights to the foreshore, the area they were being prevented from aquaculture farming, remained in Maori customary title as it had never been taken away (extinguished). It therefore followed that it could be theirs to exploit because they owned it.

The case was shifted to the Court of Appeal, where the government contested the Maori position. In its view the law was clear: when the Crown under British common law assumed sovereignty of New Zealand it claimed ownership of the foreshore and seabed regardless of existing property rights. They were to be surprised.

The 2003 Court of Appeal decision found against the Crown. The judges argued that just like other property rights, native property rights established through customary use could not be extinguished without the consent of the owners and that there was no legal reason for the foreshore and seabed to be any different. In short, these rights had not necessarily been extinguished. The judges also ruled that the place to hear these arguments was in the Maori Land Court, as it had jurisdiction over deciding whether Maori customary rights over the foreshore and seabed could convert into full property rights. Nevertheless they suggested that such rights would be difficult to establish.

None of this meant that Maori held, as of right, the ownership rights to the seabed and foreshore. But the Court of Appeal had agreed unanimously that in some very limited circumstances there was a case to be heard to test such ownership. The uncertainty created was too much for the government, and almost immediately it moved to introduce a Bill to clarify public ownership. This new Bill would deny Maori groups, including the South Island iwi and others (now formed into an umbrella organisation called Te Ope Mana a Tai), their chance to take their case to the Maori Land Court.

Such action represented a cultural and legal watershed. It was a fresh blow to Maori aspirations to use the court system to prosecute their rights and defend their interests, all the more damaging because it affected only Maori.

In reality it was the volatile context of the race relations debate at the time that prompted the government to react so defensively. But in trying to close the issue down, it achieved precisely the opposite. Had it not reacted so quickly, the government might have seized this tactical opportunity for some straight talking about a sophisticated and inclusive understanding of the Treaty, including the recognition of customary rights. Precisely because it was a moment of high tension, the public mind was focused, but at the same time it was also uncertain, polarised. Politically, the risk was too high. The expansive and inclusive discussion never got off the ground.

This was not necessarily a comfortable outcome in the public mind. If everybody was to be treated fairly under the law then Maori, like the rest of us, ought to have been able to have their day in court. The rights of ordinary citizens concerned the Crown's representatives as well. But their view was that Parliament, not the courts, was the appropriate place for this issue to be determined. The wider interests of all New Zealanders, they argued, must take precedence over the specific interests of Te Ope Mana a Tai (and all other

Maori interests to follow).

The Crown was clear from the beginning on one matter at the heart of the proposed Bill. It recognised that the new legislation would explicitly take away (or extinguish) rights that the Court of Appeal had ruled could have existed. The Crown knew it was removing the prospect that Maori (by asserting territorial customary rights) may have been able to legally prove some form of ownership, and it wanted to balance this potential loss. In return for removing the possibility of ownership, the Bill proposed that those who had lost it would be able to enter into direct discussions with the Crown over redress (not compensation). The subtlety of this distinction might not be apparent to the lay observer, but it was very clear to Maori involved in Treaty claims.

Compensation for rights lost would have required independent valuation in today's terms. It would have had a commercial edge to it, and could have been expensive for the Crown. This is not dissimilar to the way we would look for compensation under the Public Works Act if we were to lose our home to make way for a motorway. We would expect full market value for our home and some financial support for relocation. In this case the law protects us from unfair treatment. In the event of dispute, the matter is independently arbitrated and both parties are bound by this arbitration.

Not so for redress. Redress is a settlement that recognises your loss but does not value it in contemporary terms. Rather, it is a process of uneven negotiation where both parties try to agree, but the Crown ultimately determines its own ceiling. There is no appeal, no arbitration.

Money aside, at first blush the Crown's position seemed

not unreasonable. If it alone was to hold ownership of the foreshore and seabed, then this would stop anyone else claiming it — or, for that matter, selling it — Maori or Pakeha. But Pakeha were not being offered redress. Why? The answer was unavoidable. They had not lost any personal rights. Only Maori had a case to argue in law that put ownership of the foreshore under any sort of threat, and that argument was based on centuries-old understandings of customary rights and titles. These customary rights referred to the collective rights of an iwi or hapu. These were not individual or personal rights applicable to any one person.

For years Maori had been trying to use the courts and due process to have these collective rights recognised and now, in 2003, the Court of Appeal had effectively said, 'We permit you to have the matter heard and adjudicated.' Understandably, Maori were aggrieved when this permission was vetoed by the introduction of the new law.

Redress from the Crown was no done deal either. On close examination, the tests applied to determine who might be eligible for redress were going to be hard for most Maori iwi and hapu to pass. Not everybody could apply.

Maori who were directly affected — the people who saw that they had most to lose — dismissed the provisions in the Bill addressing their interests, seeing them as inappropriate and culturally minimalist. They rejected them, and they had some heavyweight support for their rejection. The Waitangi Tribunal had heard submissions on the proposed Bill in January 2004, and its members cautiously recommended that the government consider not going ahead with it in its introductory form. They suggested several ways in which the Crown could act, and none of their options reduced the capacity to arrive at a more definitive position at some later time.

Underpinning the Tribunal's view was the opportunity the Bill provided for a 'longer conversation' with all New Zealanders about the various cultural meanings around ownership. This discussion could include different views of individual and collective rights. An interim position could be established that would prevent sale or transfer of any foreshore interests, and a guaranteed right of public access for people (and shipping) while this conversation took place. The Tribunal promoted widespread public engagement in first learning about, then determining how to manage, competing cultural views. It was a considered and imaginative approach. It would deliver certainty to all parties in the short term, but it allowed for a different final result after an informed public debate, if that was what the people wanted.

Instead of this wider dialogue, the government opted for a more limited strategy of time-bound negotiation, to quarantine the issue ahead of an election year. It was interested in resolving the issues of power and control related to ownership in a way that was acceptable to the electorate. The dialogue about different cultural values would have to occur at another, less fraught time in this discussion of race. The options suggested by the Tribunal failed to impress the government, which directly criticised the Tribunal for its failure to understand the role of the Crown and its right to use Parliament to determine the will of the people.

This was not good news for the Tribunal. The Crown's decision to proceed with the Bill and pointedly reject the Tribunal's recommendations placed the credibility of the

Tribunal itself at risk. It also exposed some underlying misgivings about the role of the Tribunal, which is to provide recommendations to government about Treaty matters. It is absolutely fundamental to the Tribunal's credibility and standing that it is seen to be non-partisan. It is a bicultural body working on behalf of all New Zealanders, operating in that most difficult of conceptual spaces as interpreter and adjudicator on Maori matters, cultural and customary, for the rest of us. Because it is Maori who have the right to bring grievances before it, the Tribunal itself has become, in the public mind, a Maori forum. In fact, it is the national forum to which Maori may submit issues.

For the most part governments of all stripes have been reluctant to criticise the Tribunal because its effectiveness relies on public confidence, especially in its non-partisan nature. It is one thing to disagree with the Tribunal's findings — an entirely legitimate part of the public debate. It is another thing altogether to attack its non-partisan reputation.

We were in for a special year. As experience in 2004 was to show, with the ongoing debate over this legislation and the state of the nation address by Dr Brash, there were now well-articulated, complicated and contestable cultural and commercial interests at play on all sides. The prospect of reaching an inadequate or untimely resolution carried a high political risk for the government.

The 2004 hikoi, which culminated in over 25,000 people marching on Parliament to protest the government's proposed foreshore and seabed legislation, brought this risk home, especially in relation to the Maori constituency. But so impressive was the display of discipline, order and control exhibited by the marchers over several days that their message caught the attention of the wider public. A process of public education was occurring. In a remarkable display of cross-tribal cooperation thousands of Maori and many Pakeha from all over the country descended on Wellington to press for changes to the proposed legislation. While the Prime Minister chose not to meet them, government representatives led by Dr Michael Cullen received the formal challenge.

What eventuated was a uniquely New Zealand cultural response to addressing a major matter of civil concern. What occurred here could not have transpired in any other country in the same way, and the event itself was indicative of how far the country continues to be shaped by the interaction of Maori and non-Maori.

The area at the base of Parliament's steps assumed the physical and cultural dimensions of a marae. Although a significant police presence was in evidence, the large numbers of people in close contact with one another meant order and control was fundamentally in the hands of the participants, jointly. The mana of the leaders of all parties was on the line. On the government's flank Tariana Turia had emerged as the person most likely to take the contest to her own administration, provided she stayed. Meanwhile the balance of Labour's Maori members remained disciplined in support of their party's policy, save for Nanaia Mahuta, Labour's Tainui representative, who was reserving her position.

The resulting korero exposed the gap between the Maori expectation of a solution and the government's own perception of its room to move if it was to manage the balance of the population. Pakeha too had strong and increasingly articulate views on this matter. Much was made later of the behaviour of Tame Iti in his challenge to the Crown, using the device of spitting and snorting in the presence of the Crown representatives. Critics attacked the lack of respect shown to the Crown. As unpleasant as this may have been for sensibilities both Pakeha and Maori, it was a physical representation of the disgust many Maori felt at the legislation. It brought to mind the incident of Pakeha farmers emptying a truckload of cowpats at the door of the Department of Conservation in protest at the unfairness of the 'fart tax'. Both 'offences' fell far short of any form of physical violence or harm, and in each case the meaning of the action was unmistakable.

To the observer, the opinions exchanged across this Parliamentary foreshore seemed impossibly far apart. But something else less obvious but hugely important was also occurring. A striking feature of the interchange was the way all the participants worked with consummate skill to discuss this divisive and potentially destructive issue within a cultural construct that was neither simply Maori nor simply Pakeha, but an amalgam of the two. With such large numbers of people present, and with feelings and emotions running high, the potential for mayhem was ever present. But it did not happen.

Once again the tradition we have in this nation of freedom of political action — and indeed activism — passed the test, because the leaders of the respective participants addressed each other directly with appropriate respect. The people being led caught the sense of the occasion and followed the instructions of their leaders. All parties accepted ownership of the underlying 'rules' of this interchange. They were those of a marae engagement, albeit with much flexible adjustment to the circumstances of this particular occasion. The shape of the subsequent ritual spoke volumes about our national adaptation of our respective traditions. What could have been a calamity became a celebration of our uniqueness as a nation. This should give us confidence in the idea of a more sophisticated inclusive cultural future within our democratic tradition, if we wish to take up the challenge.

Contrasting views of the points at issue were now very clear. The hikoi had exposed the clash of world-views on the presenting take (issues). Hikoi leaders pressed the government with the challenge to amend its intended Bill to give more inclusive representation of these differing perspectives. An implicit threat was that a lack of action on the part of the government would encourage its traditional Maori support to defect. The government was equally resolute. It had a Select Committee set to hear submissions on the Bill, and it would be passed into law before Christmas.

While paying respectful heed to the demands of the hikoi Dr Cullen, on behalf of the Prime Minister, was making no promises to relent on the government's policy position, waiting instead to see what came from the submission process. This was insufficient reassurance for Tariana Turia, who resigned from Parliament and won the subsequent by-election as leader of the newly created Maori Party. Once again the leadership of Maori interests, perceived as having been thwarted by the democratic process, determined to re-engage with that same process to set about recovering their position. These were hardly the actions of separatists bent on the destruction of the State.

The hikoi excited much discussion nationwide, not all of it insightful. Under examination was a crucial question: were the cultural partners willing to trust each other sufficiently to make an accommodation that would endure? Could we see recognition of the collective rights of Maori as iwi and hapu without damage to the personal and individual rights of other New Zealanders?

A solutions-based approach

In March 2004, at a hui called at Auckland University's Waipapa Marae, I was invited by the executive of Te Ope Mana a Tai to present a Pakeha perspective on how this issue might be constructively addressed. Negotiations had been taking place between Te Ope Mana a Tai and the government in the preceding months, but had stalled. In my opening comments I suggested some rules of engagement:

> In my view we must return to the spirit and principled approach of our founding charter. Most importantly, the result must lead to the enhancement of mana of all participants. If either Treaty partner wins at the expense of the other then the issue will not be solved. What is more, all New Zealanders must be able to understand the substance of the resolution and a broad consensus will need to be gained in support. This can be no private deal between power elites. It will need popular sign-off by the people.

I explained how I took my lead from the Ngati Whatua o Orakei approach to the ownership and management of their 'whenua rangatira' parklands and foreshore. The Waitangi Tribunal had used this as one example of a solutions-based approach in a report it had just released. It is a highly successful model of joint management of a public resource by the hapu and the Auckland City Council where issues of title (including beach and foreshore), management rights and obligations are clarified to the satisfaction of all parties.

For any solution to enhance the mana of all parties, I argued, the Crown would have to acknowledge that it has not extinguished Maori customary title (or aboriginal title). It would need explicitly to recognise Maori rangatiratanga on this issue, and confirm the support provided in 1840 for the manawhenua status of Maori in regard to the foreshore and seabed. This could be done through the Maori Land Court. Tangata whenua would have to acknowledge the sovereign right of the Crown to govern, and the unfettered right of all New Zealanders to navigation and non-commercial access to the seabed and foreshore. Maori should be entitled to manage the seabed and foreshore jointly with the Crown, exercising their obligation of kaitiakitanga, which they share jointly with the Crown.

Where a possibility of commercial development of the seabed and foreshore exists, Maori would need to acknowledge that they have no more nor less rights than those accorded to all New Zealand citizens. Those with manawhenua status would need to submit to conflict of interest provisions, and abstain from voting on such matters. Any such solution, I concluded, must confirm the basic founding principle of our collective security as a nation: that we can all expect to be treated the same way under the law, and that we all have access to the law in a fair and transparent manner.

In the end all New Zealanders would know that the

commercial opportunities were exactly the same for everyone:

> Pakeha, I believe, will recognise this as fair and just. Quite simply, my experience tells me that it will only be in the exercise of true rangatiratanga, the sure confidence in your power that allows for the genius of manaaki, or generosity to the other, that will break this impasse. Such an injunction, I firmly believe, applies to both Treaty partners.

Perhaps I was too optimistic. Maori critics of this approach claimed I overestimated the Pakeha capacity for trust in this matter. In at least one instance they were right. Not long after the hikoi it was proposed that I front a commercially-sponsored campaign on prime time television about race relations. It would be focused on education about the Treaty, aimed at a Pakeha audience. The producer asked a commercially experienced 'hard head' from the advertising industry to comment on the viability of the idea. The response was clear and unequivocal:

> The pendulum has swung too far in both directions, the foreshore and seabed issue just becoming a force that swings the pendulum to the far side. I also believe issues could well be resolved with more astute Maori leadership. I think, like Pat Snedden, that Kiwis are essentially reasonable, but don't want to see the country's resources handed over to the visible face of Maoridom — whom they see as a bunch of unemployed radicals who have hijacked just causes in order to justify otherwise useless lives. Right or wrong, perception is reality.

Faced with this kind of instinctive cultural reflex, it is not hard to see that when 'we' hold the resources 'they' aren't going to get them, because 'they' can't be trusted. For many Pakeha the overwhelming fear was that if Maori controlled some of the country's resources this would lead to a calamity for the rest of New Zealand.

Such a defensive reflex is common, seen most often in business over resource management issues when corporations move to 'risk manage' the Maori problem, to reduce the inconvenience they cause or to render them irrelevant in the pursuit of the main objective. Time and again the opportunity for mutually enhanced outcomes is lost as anxiety about the unknown, focusing on what might be 'lost', drives behaviour. The government acknowledged this anxiety and assessed it as a political fact of life. Resolution required removal of the doubt while a deft attempt was made to balance competing interests, including those of Maori. This kind of balance was behind the Bill's design when it was re-introduced in November 2004 under urgency.

Preserving the status quo

Not surprisingly, the Select Committee's report back to the House was inconclusive. The thousands of submissions from the public were overwhelmingly against the Bill but the committee was so divided that they could not report a coherent recommendation. The government therefore acted on its own accord, with the support of New Zealand First, thus ensuring the necessary majority for the new Act to come into force.

Certainly Dr Cullen was clear that the problem had been effectively solved. His press release of 18 November, the day the Bill passed into law, was confident and measured. It was a lucid description of the Crown's view, under the heading: 'Certainty restored to foreshore and seabed.' An abbreviated version follows:

> New Zealanders will discover when they go to the beach this summer that the effect of the Foreshore and Seabed Bill, passed today, is to preserve the status quo. Crown ownership is confirmed and traditional rights of public access are safeguarded.
>
> Groups will be able to secure customary rights orders protecting their right to continue any activities, uses and practices they have been exercising substantially uninterrupted since 1840. This does not include customary fishing rights as these were provided for separately in the fisheries settlement.
>
> All the legislation does is to codify into statute existing common law rights. Nothing more, nothing less.
>
> Where a group can demonstrate that, but for the passage of the Bill, they would have held a Territorial Customary Right equivalent to exclusive use and occupation, they will be able to seek from the High Court the establishment of a Foreshore and Seabed Reserve or approach the Government to discuss other redress options. The reserve would acknowledge the guardianship status of the group but would also be held for the common use and benefit of all New Zealanders. These provisions were inserted at the instigation of the Maori caucus as a mechanism to both ensure Maori can have their day in court and also to recognise Maori kaitiakitanga.
>
> A lot of the anger around this issue stems from a

fundamental misconception of what the Court of Appeal actually said. It did not say Maori owned the foreshore and seabed, only that the Maori Land Court had jurisdiction to hear Maori customary land claims. And the Court made clear its views that these would be unlikely to apply to large areas.

We have been through an exhaustive process in developing the policy contained within the Foreshore and Seabed Bill. I think the final legislation provides a lasting solution and one which can take us forward as a country.

Dr Cullen's opening lines were the give-away. 'New Zealanders will discover when they go to the beach this summer that the effect of the Foreshore and Seabed Bill, passed today, is to preserve the status quo.' If things indeed were staying the same, then the new claims Maori were making must have failed.

One of Dr Cullen's predictions proved correct. New Zealanders did go to the beach over the Christmas and New Year of 2004/05 and the status quo was retained. There were few reports of disruption or controversy. The political toxicity had for the moment been excised.

But was the Bill as benign as Dr Cullen suggested? Maori would after all be able to secure customary rights orders, and if they could establish that they would have had territorial customary rights, reserves could be established or other remedies sought. This sounded like a positive response to collective rights for Maori. For the rest, was the government not merely tidying up drafting issues related to the application of the Te Ture Whenua Maori Act 1993 and simply confirming what nearly everybody understood

— that the foreshore and seabed was Crown owned?

Not everybody was so sanguine about its successful enactment. So nuanced were the technical aspects of the Bill that it was hard even for the enthusiast to gain a comprehensive and clear view of its impact. Grant Powell, counsel for Te Ope Mana a Tai, was clear.

> The final version of the Foreshore and Seabed Bill, as amended by the supplementary order paper (SOP) on 16 November 2004, far from rectifying the numerous defects identified by submitters is, if anything, even more draconian.
>
> Previous criticisms remain valid. The findings and recommendations of the Waitangi Tribunal continue to be ignored or selectively misapplied. Existing legal remedies have been removed and not only have the number of new remedies been reduced, those that remain are even more abhorrent to tikanga Maori than those contained in the previous draft, and will almost certainly prove to be expensive, unobtainable and provide nothing of substantive benefit to those holding customary rights.
>
> Further restrictions on the exercise of customary rights have emerged in the Bill, almost certainly as a result of continued unprincipled political compromise in order to seek support for the Bill. These include a requirement that applications for recognition of territorial customary rights in the High Court can only be made by those who also own the contiguous dry land, while in the case of applications for territorial customary rights and customary rights orders, no account may be taken of any spiritual or cultural association by the applicant with the area unless

that association is manifested in the physical activity or use related to a natural or physical resource.

There can be no doubt that the Bill in its present form amounts to an outright extinguishment of customary rights in the coastal marine area in a manner fundamentally at odds with the principles of the Treaty of Waitangi.

— Summary and Analysis of Amended Foreshore and Seabed Bill, SOP Tabled 16 November 2004

According to Grant Powell, the devil was in the detail. It was that detail that was going to see Maori worse off than they had been even under the status quo option prior to the introduction of this new Bill. Two examples (out of several) illustrated his point.

Clause 41(2) spells out that a customary rights order cannot be made on the basis of a 'spiritual or customary association'. It can be determined only by use rights. So matters of crucial cultural and conceptual importance to Maori which define *their* exercise of customary authority, such as manawhenua, mana moana, mana tipuna, kaitiakitanga or tino rangatiratanga, are expressly excluded by this clause. This would not be obvious to the lay observer.

Did this matter? What was its practical effect? How could non-Maori understand its significance? To illustrate the point, I thought about boats moored at Westhaven, on the Waitemata Harbour. If I (for the sake of setting out the argument) personally have a pre-existing use right, based on having moored my boat there for years, then that use right would continue into the future. What is more, for a fee I could probably transfer it to someone else.

But if my group claimed a right to moor our boats there,

based on the history of my relatives having given explicit permission to others for hundreds of years to also secure their boats at certain times within certain seasons, or if my relatives had at various times explicitly prohibited the use of such moorings because of death on the water, or shortage of certain stock for fishing, thus demonstrating that we controlled these waters, would our claim for customary use rights be valid today?

If I understood Grant Powell, the theoretical answer would be probably not. And certainly not if the practices described above had not been substantially the same and uninterrupted since 1840 — even if the reason for that interruption had been found to be the illegal actions of the Crown. The phrase used most often by the Tribunal was to be 'in breach of solemn undertakings'. Regardless of circumstances, if there had been a marked break of many years since 1840 in my family's continued occupation, my application for customary usage rights would not pass the test.

Similarly, it was Powell's assessment that Maori would have serious difficulty in establishing their loss of territorial customary rights (separate from the customary use rights) covered by this Bill. This was important because it would entitle them to ask for the provision of reserves, or to negotiate redress.

The law seemed reasonable enough on the face of it, allowing for such negotiation to take place. But Powell was not confident. He argued that the tests iwi will have to pass to exercise this option are substantial. Not the least of these is the requirement that no claim can be made for the foreshore unless the tribal group owned the 'contiguous land' alongside as per clause 28(2). In short, if you didn't own the land up to the beaches there would be no grounds for asserting a territorial customary right over the foreshore. That was the case even if your iwi or hapu had maintained continuous manawhenua status by virtue of occupation in the rohe since 1840. As Powell concluded:

> From a practical point of view, this creates insurmountable difficulties for any applicant. In most parts of the country those holding customary rights to the foreshore and seabed simply do not own the contiguous land.

Once again it was difficult to see the bridging points in the arguments. Only the effective testing of the propositions over time would shed light on that assessment. The answer might well reside with the Courts. They will decide how to interpret Parliament's intentions on the facts of each case in front of them.

So have we solved the dilemma I posed at the outset?

Well, clearly the ownership issue is now certain — the Crown owns the foreshore and seabed. In this respect concerns over continued public access to the foreshore, both real and imagined, have been contained. And there can be no sale of remaining coastal marine land in public ownership except with parliamentary approval. In this respect the personal rights of all New Zealanders have been clarified.

But what of the Article 2 collective rights of Maori, protective of te tino rangatiratanga? The law provides for redress if it can be proven that such rights — such as territorial customary rights — have been lost. Thus it is explicit that rights may have been taken and that some quid pro quo is required.

Herein lies the Act's substantial weakness: what has been chosen is a minimal, incremental option in the recognition of Article 2 Maori rights. The Act concentrates on how to make up for what has been lost, rather than legislating for what may have been gained. The government has taken a politically calibrated 'risk reduction' position, not an expansionary or inclusive approach, and the disadvantaged party is once again Maori, not as individuals, but as collectives in their iwi and hapu.

It could have been so different.

The agreement reached between Ngati Whatua o Orakei and the Auckland City Council is but one way that the challenge could have been addressed, and all parties could have benefited. That solution is a profoundly Treaty-based agreement where the rangatiratanga of Ngati Whatua is protected as Article 2 requires, and where the distinct world-views of both hapu and council have their place and co-exist in the pursuit of negotiated common goals.

In contrast, the current risk-adverse stance cannot endure. This is not because it is minimal or malicious, but because it is so utterly out of step with the emerging knowledge of our history and the examples all around us of new possibilities in the way we do things. There is just too much to be gained for all New Zealanders by taking a more expansive view. With the avalanche of new historical writing available to us since the 1970s we will soon all have a more sophisticated understanding of the founding agreement that launched our nation. It is already happening, and it will continue because it is fundamental to building a more inclusive society.

For now, the passing of this latest law suggests that such a possibility remains out of reach. But as the Maori population continues to grow at a faster rate than any other ethnic grouping, and their continued renaissance unfolds, it cannot remain so. As a more sophisticated understanding of Article 2 obligations takes hold more New Zealanders will see the need to react positively, not defensively, to Maori aspirations. It is my view that this legislation will be revisited within the next generation.

9 : Imagining the future with Article 2

From Treaty truth-telling to Treaty fulfilment

There is a news report in the *New Zealand Herald* (incorporating the *Southern Cross*) of March 1933 of a hui celebrating ninety-two years since the 1841 landing of Governor Hobson at Okahu Bay. He had been greeted and provided with land by Ngati Whatua on his journey to establish this nation's capital in Auckland. At that 1933 hui were two elderly kaumatua in their nineties, both of whom had been present on the original occasion in 1841. Also present was a young boy, just six years old, whose birth name was Ian Hugh Paora. Two years earlier, exercising their ancient prerogative, his elders had renamed him Ian Hugh Kawharu, after Paora Kawharu, the boy's great-grandfather and a nineteenth-century Ngati Whatua chief. Today Sir Hugh Kawharu chairs the Ngati Whatua o Orakei Maori Trust Board.

This little vignette captures a microcosm of our nation's joint history. So fresh is the writing on the Treaty that there are some alive today who directly knew people who were present (even as young children) circa 1840. And there are customs practised today, such as naming children after ancestors, that date from well before the Treaty. So when some of us talk of the Treaty in terms of 'that was then and this is now', it is worth reflecting on what we are saying. The 'then' and the 'now' are inextricably joined.

The relative immediacy of the Treaty signing is our great national advantage. In many countries, 160 years is a small blip on the radar. Having something of a long view about this will be helpful. After thirty years of Tribunal hearings it is now indisputable that the protection of te tino rangatiratanga as guaranteed under Article 2 has, in historical terms, been adjudged seriously flawed. The evidence abounds. The jury is no longer out.

When we recognise this truth we become alert to a question that is central to our future national identity. It is a question, some would say, of profound moral dimensions.

Having settled claims for past injustices, how and why should we recognise Maori collective rights (and obligations) into the future? We need to be clear-headed about this.

If Maori have been systematically disenfranchised of their Article 2 rights (and therefore unable to fulfil their obligations) then the benefits of that dispossession have, by definition, gone to non-Maori. Clearly nobody alive today (either Maori or non-Maori) can be blamed for allowing such historical dispossession to occur, or be held responsible for making good the loss. That is why we have invented the Waitangi Tribunal. It is our way of ensuring that the State bears the responsibility on behalf of us all for both acknowledging and remedying the wrong done. In international terms, this is an unprecedented solution of genius proportions, but it meets only half the challenge.

The other aspect of the moral challenge is precisely to resist the 'that was then and this is now' scenario. Why should we need to do this? Not simply because it is an insular and barren response to creating an informed and inclusive nationhood, but because it won't work. The clear truth is that on the Maori side of our population the renaissance is underway. Maori are making gains as individual citizens in every aspect of public life, and the rate of improvement is accelerating.

Just as crucially, gains in collective or tribal identity are also being established. Herein lies a key understanding for Pakeha and the Crown in this process. This is all about the recovery and affirmation of manawhenua. When Ngai Tahu began its Treaty negotiations in the mid-1980s, they claimed 6000 identified beneficiaries linked by known whakapapa. Today they have over 30,000 on their list. Quite possibly these people are simply attracted by potential dividends. But it is more likely that the rising profile of the tribal administration regarding their Treaty claim, as well as pride over their substantial financial success, has had a positive effect in once again encouraging Ngai Tahu people to identify with their own iwi roots.

This is not a far-fetched idea. In February 2005 I spoke at a conference in Alexandra, in Central Otago. Two speakers thanked me for my contribution, both of them eloquent and gracious. One, a Pakeha pensioner, said he had met only one Maori during his school days. The other, a young Maori in his thirties, commented that Maori make up 12 per cent of the population in the Southland region. Such is the gulf in cultural perception across generations of New Zealanders.

Today's reality is that South Island Maori are no longer invisible. Their profile is being transformed through the exercise of rangatiratanga by the newly constituted Ngai Tahu tribal administration. Crucial to this is their identification of their manawhenua status over their traditional tribal areas. This is where the claim process has been so useful to Maori. No longer are they excluded from resource management issues or without representation on various government agencies. They now have a degree of State and public recognition as a tribal collective (iwi) that they have not experienced for over a century. They are present when decisions are being made and, like it or not, their collective voice is getting a hearing and is being considered. To exclude their collective voice is no longer politically tenable or legally possible. Their successful Treaty settlements enshrine by Act of Parliament their manawhenua status for future dealings with the Crown. It cannot be dismissed.

And this same effect is being felt in every area where tribal groups have resolved their claims with the Crown. Over the next generation, as final claims are signed off, this will be true for the whole of New Zealand. For those irritated by the realisation that their old mate Stephen has suddenly become Tipene, consider first the details of the Ngai Tahu story as documented in their claim. Any thoughts of contemporary opportunism need to be carefully weighed against the historical fact of near cultural extinction. A less jaundiced judgement might suggest this is a time to celebrate the genuine recovery of cultural identity and to be jointly proud of it, as a nation.

But what's in it for the rest of New Zealand? Quite a bit, actually. The sorry facts are that Maori, notwithstanding their cultural renaissance, are still at the bottom in a whole raft of adverse social statistics. They represent in many Pakeha minds a threatening underclass, capable of destabilising our march toward increasing prosperity. In many areas of our public life, business, crime and politics, Maori appear more often on the radar as a risk to be managed than as an opportunity to be embraced. The most public exception to this perception is sport, where precisely the opposite is true.

How do we address and possibly reverse much of this negative reality, and what relevance has Article 2 to this reversal?

Accepting the need for a different approach

Looking at the development of kaupapa Maori (Maori for Maori) processes is one of the answers. At a crude level many non-Maori New Zealanders find this idea offensive. It suggests separatism, ethnic preference — or worse, an exclusion of ourselves.

We need to stand back from this gut-level reaction and consider the evidence. Most existing kaupapa Maori services do include non-Maori as part of their client base. Their numbers are often a critical part of a service's financial viability. They are not ethnic-exclusive. Further, we need to be careful not to miss a key point. If we continue to do what we are doing at the moment, and to fail as we are currently failing, should the obvious thing not be to ask for a different approach? The answer is not further welfare penalty, taking away for adoption babies from young mothers and fathers who have been sexually careless, or imposing harsher penalties or longer sentences for crime. For Maori at least, one answer must be to seek solutions within collective Maori frameworks resourced to own the problem.

If today we took a sophisticated view of applying our understanding of Article 2 of the Treaty, we might decide that support for kaupapa Maori approaches is an unfulfilled obligation owed to our Treaty partners, and that we would be better off resourcing them to get on with it. I am talking here about covering the full range of public interventions: social services, social housing, health services, family services, crime prevention, education and welfare. In short, the whole gamut of activities we describe as support service delivery in New Zealand.

There ought to be options for kaupapa Maori service delivery in all these areas, and they ought to be sustainably resourced. However, there must be a balance. That balance relates to the quid pro quo of such a deliberate policy departure. There can be no recognition of mana (power and control) without the requirement for manaakitanga (hospitality to the other).

Intrinsic to the resourcing of the exercise of rangatiratanga is the requirement for reciprocity (utu): a reciprocity from iwi that involves not only the competent, accountable and efficient delivery of the services, but which exhibits *full and collective* ownership of the problems being addressed. This kind of concept goes beyond the notion that social miscreants are solely the masters of their own destiny, good or bad. That works on the basis that risks and rewards are the same for everyone, no matter what their history. The empirical evidence is overwhelming that this is simply not true.

For too many Maori, the historical reality of collective tribal decimation is a profound psychological counter to the idea of a 'level playing field' for all. Recovery of that collective centre, by knowing who you are and where you belong, increases the chances of personal cultural coherence. Thus, providing options that Maori iwi and hapu can deliver for their own people goes to the heart of the personal search for collective belonging. This is not a short-term exercise but a profound reorientation of the way we as a nation deal with the issues that undermine our national unity and prosperity.

This kind of thinking is not foreign to us. In the early 1970s the Catholic population was agitating for State aid for private schools. Their argument was not unlike what I am proposing here. In effect, Catholics were saying that it was not appropriate to insist that the 'special character' of their schools was a matter of personal belief, and therefore outside the requirement for public support. They wanted the power and control to educate their children within their own accepted 'meaning system' and to have that supported by the State. They argued that Catholics paid their taxes like any other people, and were now effectively paying twice for their children's education which, for the best part of a century, had not been supported by government money.

Critics attacked the policy as preferential treatment for Catholics. The Catholics responded by saying that it was a century of religious exclusion that had prevented them from being resourced to run their own schools as should always have been their right. In the event, the argument succeeded. The Crown and Catholic education authorities negotiated a settlement that allowed for the 'integration' of their schools so that they would receive the same funding as State schools, in return for agreed restrictions to the proportion of non-Catholic pupils on the roll. This assuaged in good measure the lobbyists from the public system who were opposed to the new policy, for fear it might undermine the roll numbers at their own schools. Today the waiting lists for Catholic schools are long as people are attracted to the coherent 'meaning system' of that tradition.

One might ask, if this kind of thinking and flexibility in policy is good enough for a religious minority, might it not also be appropriate for a Treaty partner?

Pakeha might fairly be suspicious about such a systematic departure from the status quo. Many New Zealanders are all too familiar with the media reports of Maori provider failure in many areas, of fraud committed against trust boards or individuals acting in their own interests to the detriment of the collective. The face of drug and alcohol abuse and personal violence is often seen as Maori. So too, family dysfunction is perceived as disproportionately a Maori problem. Many Maori don't trust their own iwi/hapu service delivery because they see incompetence, minimal confidentiality, self-interest for private gain, poor staff relationships, personal aggrandisement or even inter-tribal prejudice. Often there is little confidence in the leadership. These feelings are so strong that they would rather receive their services from outside the tribal constructs. And they should be able to do just that. This is not about narrowing the choice for

Maori but about increasing the possibilities for successful intervention, no matter what the medium.

However, the picture of successful Maori service delivery is far from bleak. There are health and education providers and commercial operations which are among the top in their field. Ngati Porou Hauora runs all health services on the East Coast, inclusive of secondary hospital services, and is accredited nationwide to the highest standards. Mai FM, commercial radio owned by Te Runanga o Ngati Whatua, is this country's highest-rating music station. It is operating in a fiercely competitive radio market that is dominated by two multinationals. With a fraction of their capital base it has captured the youth market in Auckland. Likewise Ngai Tahu has shown huge financial acumen in its business activities, making it one of the highest-performing corporates in New Zealand. Maori incorporations are some of the highest-achieving farming businesses we have.

Te Wananga o Aotearoa, while the subject of much controversy and adverse scrutiny, has had stellar success with the introduction of Maori to tertiary-level education, and its promotion of te reo Maori has been second to none in our educational institutions. No other tertiary institution has achieved such levels of take-up by Maori of tertiary educational options in the whole of our educational history. It would be wrong to ignore its impact on Maori while aspects of its governance are being minutely examined.

This is not an unrealistically rosy view. For every first-rate success, there are many failures. But the frequency of those failures is not helped by the 'ambiguous climate' in which many organisations operate. I have seen Maori organisations being asked to 'tone down' their Maori analysis so as not to frighten the horses, most often the Crown funding agency. I have never seen this happen to Pakeha organisations. It is as if the support for the Maori collective approach is acceptable, provided the funder doesn't become agitated. Thus Article 2 exploration of rights is permissible, provided you whisper. If you shout, the money dries up.

There are also massive Maori skill deficits in all sorts of critical areas — not least in tikanga Maori. Consider for a moment the forty years lost for Ngati Whatua o Orakei between the burning of the marae in 1951 and the passing of the 1991 Act that gave Bastion Point back to the hapu. In that period nearly two generations of tikanga practice were relegated to private garages for tangi, and there was almost no public engagement with either the State or other Maori iwi or hapu. The ability to host hui nearly disappeared. Only the resilience of the people retained the vestiges of their cultural taonga. The fact that they are fully functional in their Ngati Whatuatanga (Ngati Whatua cultural behaviour) is a minor miracle. Yet the recovery of their cultural practices gives vital confidence to their programme of collective revitalisation. It is the very underpinning of their restoration. They are actively training their own people for the task of self-management ahead of them, and second best is not a concept that will sit easily with this hapu.

The message from this experience is straightforward. We simply have to get beyond the scandal value of supposed preferential funding for Maori, just as the argument for funding of integrated schools for Catholic and non-Catholic alike was eventually accepted. Our arrival point must be a mature understanding of the benefits of the affirmation of Article 2. We need together, Maori and Pakeha, to determine in our public affairs how support for rangatiratanga can be applied in contemporary terms. If Maori are appropriately resourced and collectively agree to take ownership of the problem caused by historical social and cultural dislocation, the chances of an enduring solution increase exponentially.

'Owning' the problem

This is a journey. There is no one answer. In some circumstances Maori may say, 'We cannot do what you ask of us because the capacity of our iwi at present to "own the problem" does not exist.'

But I am confident that the overwhelming response from Maori will be to take up the challenge. Released from the constant burden of having to convince the State to recognise their rangatiratanga, Maori will mobilise to address the root causes of the social underclass that so vexes us. This will be a long process. My experience with Ngati Whatua o Orakei after the return of Bastion Point suggests that within fifteen years we will be able to identify clear and positive progress. Within a generation we will see transformation.

How difficult is this journey? Fortunately the resources we have available to meet this challenge are substantial. At this point a national inventory of our advantages might be useful.

We now have a huge historical base to draw on. This is a great advantage, provided we see it reflected in our school system. The challenge for the twenty-first-century school-age child is to gain a grasp of the new history written in the last thirty years, by historians and through the Tribunal process. By not knowing our history, we got ourselves into strife in our race relations. We don't have to repeat that mistake.

We are in the midst of an economic boom of sustained proportions. The rates of Maori unemployment are the lowest since pre-1970. There is more social housing and health care aimed at improving Maori life-span than ever before. Maori entry into business, entrepreneurial activity and self-employment is at an all-time high. With surpluses at record levels, the opportunity intentionally to realign the delivery of public intervention for Maori is fundable as never before.

The level of social awareness around the issues of Treaty application is rising rapidly. After Dr Brash's 2004 Orewa speech there was an initial outbreak of Pakeha angst that support for Maori had gone too far. Longer reflection on this is changing people's minds. There is now, in my experience, a willingness to get to the heart of this matter. The discussion has opened us up and the reflections are promising. We are becoming more informed and better equipped to deal with the wider issues.

There is a cultural renaissance of Maori, largely supported and appreciated by non-Maori. We sing our national anthem in Maori and English without reserve. Our Maori artists, filmmakers, commercial and sporting heroes are now representative of 'more of us' than ever before. There are record numbers of Maori Members of Parliament, and a new Maori party is an expression of a self-confidence not seen previously. Our cultural processes are adapting, as the response to last year's hikoi so eloquently demonstrated. We are discovering ways of being a New Zealander that are not solely Maori or Pakeha, but an amalgam of the two.

Similarly, there are now successful working models of the way things can be done. The kohanga reo movement demonstrates a competently run te reo (Maori language) preschool service. The areas in which it struggles are the same as those where the education department struggles with general programmes, where scale is small and expertise is scarce. There are Maori public health programmes focusing on smoking cessation that are achieving substantial gains with at-risk Maori mothers. Maori language television, after a shaky start, is now well launched. Without question it will need lots of support to sustain vigour, audience reach and programme excellence. It has substantial commercial challenges, but in comparison it requires from the government only a fraction of the resources provided to State-run television when it began.

For all our difficulties, there is something approaching political fairness in Aotearoa/New Zealand. It is more of an orientation than a fully achieved reality, but it is there. The foreshore law may be flawed but it represents a genuine attempt, albeit incremental, to recognise that there needs to be a way of accommodating the competing aspirations of different sections of our nation. To the extent that the Act represents the fruit of a kind of 'political panic' about race relations it showed how far we have still to go to become confident and trust each other cross-culturally. But to leave it at that would be to ignore the fact that the legislation did attempt to address customary practices that did not derive from Anglo-Saxon roots. We can all count that as a minor triumph of national self-confidence.

The decision to create the Waitangi Tribunal in 1975 and to extend its brief in 1985 to address grievances dating from 1840 was an act of enormous courage and insight. This represents a milestone in our history, comparable to the Treaty signing itself, the right of women to vote and the creation of the welfare state. This is an achievement without parallel in the world. It is incomprehensible that a people with this much good sense, intuitive courage and insight into the healing of human affairs related to its indigenous people will lose its nerve when confronting new challenges on this path. We now have a legacy of direct dealing even when faced with the painful truth, and we are the stronger for it.

Finally, and importantly, we have time. The 160 years since the signing of the Treaty is indeed a blip on the radar of history, including our own. If we accept that New Zealand has been occupied since 1300, then our difficulties with the Treaty have only been in the most recent quarter of this occupation. This is not so far distant that they cannot be remedied.

If the generation since 1975 may be described as the 'Treaty truth-telling' generation, let the next be the 'Treaty fulfilment' generation. Undoubtedly, we will all be better off for it.

Glossary

hapu
sub-tribe of an iwi

hikoi
step, deputation in support of an issue or for a defined purpose

iwi
tribal grouping

kaitiakitanga
guardianship over resources

kaupapa
goal, purpose or agenda

kohanga reo
full immersion Maori language preschool

koiwi
human remains

korero
speech, discussion, talk

kura kaupapa
full immersion Maori language primary and secondary school

mana
  authority and control that encompasses honour, dignity and respect in the way it is exercised
manaakitanga
  obligation to offer appropriate hospitality, consideration for others
manawhenua
  tribal authority within a region (rohe)
Maori
  descendant(s) of tangata whenua
marae
  meeting place, locus of tribal mana
maramataka
  Maori seasonal calendar
moko
  tattoo
Pakeha
  descendants of settlers from Britain and Europe
Pakehatanga
  Pakeha cultural manners, behaviour and beliefs
papakainga
  settlement
rangatiratanga
  chiefly authority exercising trusteeship over taonga
rohe
  tribal region
runanga
  tribal council
taiaha
  spear, weapon
take
  an issue, cause, reason
tangata Tiriti
  non-Maori who belong to the land by right of the Treaty

GLOSSARY

tangata whenua
Maori, first people of the land (modern)

tangi, tangihanga
ritual farewell of the dead, funeral wake

taniwha
mythical water monster used metaphorically to signal danger/disorder in relationships

taonga
sacred tribal treasures both material and non-material

tauiwi
descendant(s) of all non-Maori, includes Pakeha and immigrants

tikanga
cultural manners, beliefs, practices, customs

tupapaku
deceased person

tupuna
ancestor(s)

urupa
burial site(s)

wairua
spirit, also spiritual sense of well-being within a kin-based group

whakapapa
genealogy by ancestral connection

whenua
land

whenua rangatira
noble/chiefly land, undisputed ownership and control